How to Land the Perfect Internship in International Relations

Your Guide to Succeeding in the Field

CONTRIBUTORS:

Madaleine Domingo
Erin Dwyer
Deniz Guzeldere
Ryan Haile
Amanda Mueller

Saleena Ordorica
Randy Reyes
Sabrina Richards
Namie Yazaki

DEDICATION

Thank you to Dr. Avi Spiegel for your leadership in creating this project, and for your guidance and encouragement. We could not have done it without you!

NOTE FROM THE EDITORS

Have you ever wanted a roadmap for how to think about internships, how to secure one, and how to successfully execute one? These remarkable MAIR students have come together to bring you this book - a collection of personal experience, tips, and tricks for how to bring this all together! We are so excited to showcase our own internship knowledge and experience with the hope that our journeys will help future interns be successful.

Madaleine Domingo and Randy Reyes
San Diego, California

CONTENTS

Part Two: The Keys to Success

ACKNOWLEDGMENTS

Thank you to the University of San Diego, the College of Arts and Sciences, and the Master of Arts in International Relations program for teaching us, students, about the book publishing process. This allowed us to learn more about publishing, while also highlighting our valuable internship experiences. Additionally, we would like to express our gratitude to Dr. Avi Spiegel for organizing the class and facilitating this unique opportunity. Many thanks to our peer, Zoe Knepp, who kindly supported us with the design, layout, and organization of the book. Lastly, we would like to thank all of the organizations that granted our internship opportunities. We hope our unique backgrounds and experiences inspire students studying international relations to pursue internships that align with their values, career aspirations, and future endeavors.

FOREWORD
All Internships Are Local

International relations professors have answers to many questions — except for one.

When students come to see us in our offices on campus, they ask us about the classes we're teaching. They ask about the readings on the syllabus or about how to prepare for class. On many occasions they ask about their grades: about what is going to be on the next exam, or about their performance on the last exam.

But of all the questions students come to ask professors of politics, one is posed just as often as any other – but it is one we know little about.

How can I find a good internship?

This book serves as an antidote to that ignorance.

When my nine students in a graduate level professional development course in international relations surveyed the scholarly landscape – conducting a literature review of work on internships – they found a glaring hole. For all the talk on college campuses about internships – about their importance, their necessity, their pros, their cons – no one had set out to distill all this competing and conflicting information into a single volume. Sure, there were blogs and pamphlets and websites and advice columns, but there was no single book that students could pick up that would help them.

This volume does just that. It systematically tackles every aspect of the internship issue, from the search to the successful completion, from the categorizations of internships to the ethics behind them.

This book will serve as a critical guide for students – and also for professors and parents. Think of it as a toolkit for anyone who has considered an internship, who desires an internship or who already has one and wants to excel at it. Campus career service offices will also find this guide useful. In it, these nine experts -- students who have sought, and successfully completed internships – write with clarity and authority about the ins and outs of the internship process.

But this book is about a lot more than the typical internship. One fundamental challenge for students interested in obtaining work experience in the field of global politics is the challenge of travel. This was made even more acute during the pandemic, when students were stuck at home or on campus. Many students believe that internships in the field are simply impossible without engaging in expensive and time consuming travel. This volume interrogates and ultimately disproves this misconception. These student authors gained important and valuable experience in international relations without ever leaving the city of San Diego.

How did they do this? Through their ingenuity and perseverance, they sought out jobs with international dimensions right here in San Diego. One worked with immigrant communities; one with a member of Congress; one with law enforcement; one with the US Department of State (virtually); one with a multinational corporation whose profits exceed the GDP of many countries; one with an organization that elevates the voices of BIPOC communities around the world; one with a public interest law firm that works with asylum seekers; and, finally, two students worked with diplomacy and world affairs organizations in the city.

These students showed us all that there is much to gain – and learn – from the communities around us. To borrow from the late Speaker of the House Tip O'Neil: all internships are local!

The Book

The book is broken up into nine chapters, organized into three parts. Part One is called "Navigating the Search." It introduces readers to the topic of internships: what they are and how to navigate the diverse and changing landscapes. Part Two, "The Keys to Success," offers important lessons for excelling at all internships at the highest levels. Part Three – "Vital Perspectives" – considers viewpoints and debates that are often overlooked.

The book begins with an overview first chapter by Randy Reyes that introduces readers to the subject and draws on his remarkable internship experience with the Office of Immigrant Affairs, City of San Diego. The next two chapters take readers on a tour of internships in both the public and private sectors. Amanda Mueller, drawing on her experience interning with the Sheriff's Department in San Diego, discusses in Chapter 2 how to conduct a search for an internship in the public sector. Next, Ryan Haile writes in Chapter 3 about the process of acquiring an internship in the private sector, drawing on his internship with one of the country's largest multinational tech companies, Qualcomm, which is headquartered in San Diego.

Part Two spells out the "Keys to Success" for any intern. Sabrina Richards kicks off this second part of the book with a definitive and immensely readable guide to internship success. Sabrina interned for a member of the U.S. Congress and shares, in Chapter 4, everything she knows about how to crush the day to day. Note to students: read this chapter carefully; you won't regret it! Next, in Chapter 5, Madeleine Domingo, a successful intern with the U.S. Department of State, takes applicants inside the interview process, lending indispensable advice for how to handle each part of this often opaque process. Finally, Saleena Ordorica tackles, in Chapter 6, the critical element of networking. Saleena has tremendous experience in the area from her internship with The San Diego World Affairs Council, a novel organization that hosts visiting diplomats and delegations from all over the world!

Part Three begins with Namie Yazaki. As an international student from Japan, Namie persevered through the internship process – and the often labyrinthine process of obtaining the right proper visa – on her own. After her successful internship with an organization that promotes BIPOC communities, Namie wrote Chapter 7 to help other similarly situated students. Now, no international student seeking an internship in the United States will have to go at it alone. Next, in Chapter 8, drawing on her experience with the

San Diego Diplomacy Council, Deniz Guzeldere skillfully investigates the all important debate over paid vs unpaid internships: are unpaid internships ethical? Is there any value to them? Finally, in the perfect closing chapter, Chapter 9, Erin Dwyer uses the very interview skills she honed from her experience with the Southern California Immigration Project to hear from interns themselves. By conducting, condensing, and then cogently analyzing interviews about the internship process, Erin gives readers a rare glimpse into the life of interns.

The Contributors

This foreword would not be complete without a brief word about this special group of student contributors. All are students at the University of San Diego and all are students in our globally recognized Master's in International Relations (MAIR) program. Almost all were admitted to our cutting edge combined degree program which allows students to begin graduate school while still undergrads—and then complete the MA during a fifth year. The combined BA/MA degree allows advanced students to dip their toes into graduate level work – with coursework on topics ranging from diplomacy in the 21st Century to strategic studies to Energy Politics in Latin America. One is a different kind of joint degree student, in our MA/JD dual degree program with the USD School of Law.

Any book would be lucky to have these remarkable seven contributors and two editors. It was certainly a team effort: Amanda, Erin, Namie, and Saleena, Erin worked on the design team. Deniz, Ryan and Sabrina gave extra assistance to proofreading. Sabrina played a key role in adding pizzazz to each chapter. The terrific book cover was designed by one of our authors, Erin. Another MAIR student, Zoe Knepp, did all the book layout work and she deserves our tremendous gratitude.

I want to give special credit to the two editors of this volume: Madaleine Domingo and Randy Reyes. Maddy and Randy worked tirelessly on behalf of this book, and it simply would not have been possible without them. They conceptualized the shape of the book, organized countless meetings, kept their fellow students to a deadline, and always made sure to follow up with them—and me. And, of course, they played an active role in organizing our fabulous book launch party (replete with a fresh churro ice cream sandwich bar)!

Maddy and Randy weren't just fantastic editors of an exciting book about internships; they were, like all our authors, terrific interns. As my students know I like to say: the proof is in the pudding! Randy parlayed his internship with the Office of Immigrant Affairs for the City of San Diego into a job with San Diego City Council. Maddy parlayed her work with the US Department of State and Education USA Russia into a prestigious Fulbright Scholarship to Thailand!

The Setting

Our MA in International relations (MAIR) program is a selective program that focuses on small seminars and has an incredible student-faculty ratio, with a diverse selection of attentive faculty—leading scholars and former Ambassadors and admirals who love to teach. We are among the only seminar-based MA in International Relations in Southern California. It would be rare to find a program where teaching is undertaken more seriously.

Nestled between the border and the beach, between Mexico and the Pacific Ocean, San Diego is an ideal spot to study international relations. As a bridge to the Pacific Rim and with our strong military presence (Navy SEALs train just down the coast), there are not many places in the country that match this globally oriented location.

We've always known that San Diego is a great spot to study international relations. Now, with the publication of this book, we now know it is a tremendous place to do internships in international relations.

In closing, I would like to thank the organizations that sponsored our interns: The Office of Immigrant Affairs, City of San Diego; the San Diego Sheriff's Office; Qualcomm; The

Office of U.S. Representative Darrel Issa; The U.S. Department of State; The San Diego World Affairs Council; Children's Advocacy Institute; Southern California Immigration Project; ASCENDtials; and The San Diego Diplomacy Council.

I hope you all enjoy reading and using this book as much as I enjoyed working on it with these students. I will keep many copies on my bookshelf. And when students in future years come to my office to ask me about internships, I now know what to do: I will quickly get up from my chair and grab a copy of this book. These chapters by these amazing and accomplished student authors will be able to help prospective interns more than any faculty member ever could.

Avi Spiegel, J.D., Ph.D.
Associate Professor of Political Science and International Relations and
Director of Graduate Programs in International Relations
University of San Diego
San Diego, California

PART ONE

Navigating the Search

I
KICK-STARTING A CAREER: WHY AN INTERNSHIP?
Randy Reyes

Roadmap:
i. Introduction
ii. The Relationship Between Types of Internships and Post-Internship Opportunities
iii. The Network and the Future
iv. The Digital Network and the Future
v. Conclusion

Key Takeaways:
- Internships are key for successful professional development in individuals with dreams and aspirations for a better future.
- In the field of government, politics, and international relations, who one knows is KEY.
- Your professional network is the group of people in your life that help you find professional growth, new opportunities, and development.
- Job procurement is one of the most important reasons to do an internship, in addition to transferring the skills learned.
- Establishing and maintaining a network is of high importance for one's future, and the same can be said about a digital network.

"...who one knows is KEY."

Why Should I Consider Getting an Internship? It's Your First Step Towards the Future!

Internships are vital to the professional development of all, especially when it pertains to one's dreams, aspirations, and choice of study. For example, for a student studying international relations, global studies, political science, public policy, or any other topic that prepares one for careers in the public service sector, obtaining an internship in this sector is essential for one's future after the completion of their studies. Ultimately, the type of internship one selects is important to where one finds eventual employment. Internships can vary in tasks including research, preparation of informational memorandums (memos), clerical responsibilities, project assistance, or more. These internships are offered by both the public and private sectors, and are different depending on the organization or institution. Some internship programs better prepare interns, as they allow for interns to be more involved with projects and major assignments, while others simply task interns to be assistants or "observers," which hinders a more enriching experience. But again, this depends on the organization and the supervisors at each individual internship program. In this chapter, I will dive into the various types of internships and how these lead to employment opportunities, the different types of opportunities, and the importance of a professional network.

What Kind of Internship Should I Get? Depends on Your Interests! Do Your homework to Find Out the Options.

As previously stated, there are a plethora of different types of majors and programs, all of which mostly teach the overarching themes of political science and public service, but that also have specific concentrations designed to educate those with specific interests and professional aspirations. Such majors and programs might influence one's decision as to what type of work one wants to do and what type of internship one wants to obtain. For instance, a student that is interested in US-Mexico relations, politics in Mexico, and Latin American relations at large will be more likely to be inclined to find an internship with an organization that works on these topics. But even within these topics, there are options as to what types of internships are available for students. This can include an internship with a research group or think tank that is largely focused on conducting research on such topics to prepare reports and conduct workshops. This type of organization is one that is within the private sector also known as an NGO, but can also be found in the public sector within a government office at the local, state, or federal level. The next sections of this chapter will include a diverse set of internship examples for students to understand the various options available.

Option 1: Opportunities Involving Research:

To be consistent with the example described, an example of a research group that concentrates on politics in Mexico and US-Mexico relations would be *Justice in Mexico* (JIM). JIM is an organization based out of the University of San Diego. It "works to improve citizen security, strengthen the rule of law, and protect human rights in Mexico" (justiceinmexico.org). More specifically, they conduct research to promote robust and informed conversations, and work on providing solutions and policy recommendations to address such nuanced issues that impact the Mexican judicial and political systems. These types of organizations can typically be found on university campuses, given that universities are research centers.

An internship with this type of organization would most likely consist of conducting research and assisting the research group with collecting data and information for their reports, and would prepare a student interested in advancing a career in policy research, policy analysis, or even academia. While this is a private sector job, it is an internship that is much more research focused, and can prepare one to continue in the research sector or perhaps transition into a public service role, working for a policy maker or policy making institution analyzing policies, or putting together reports to draft new policies. For example, working for an office like the *City of San Diego's, Office of the Independent Budget Analyst* (IBA), which is an office designed to "annually review and analyze the Mayor's Proposed Budget, and to publish a detailed report of the analysis within two weeks of the release of the budget" (City of San Diego, Office of the Independent Budget Analyst). Additionally, this office is tasked with reviewing all items presented before the legislative body, including the City Council and the San Diego Housing Authority to analyze such proposed policies that are aligned with the City's budget, finances, and the finances of other municipal governmental bodies. Essentially, this office conducts serious policy analysis and research to make fiscal recommendations to the City Council, San Diego Housing Authority, and the City's Chief Executive, the Mayor. Such a role requires extensive research skills and interests, therefore, an internship that provides these skills and experience would prepare an individual for a role with an organization like the City of San Diego's Office of the IBA. Again, this is just an example of the many policy analysts type roles that exist across the world both in the private and public sector.

Option 2: Opportunities with the Federal Government:

A second option for a student interested in US-Mexico relations, politics in Mexico, and Latin American relations at large would be to intern in the public sector for a governmental institution. This can include a job at the federal level most likely with a Congressperson who represents a district at the border or at the local level with a border City. To illustrate this further, a federal example for an internship would be interning for the Office of Congressman Juan Vargas. Why his office? Because Congressman Vargas is the one Congressional representative from the San Diego Congressional Delegation who represents border communities like Otay Mesa and San Ysidro that live along the San Diego border. This information can be found by doing thorough research on the elected official. If one is interested in working for a Congressperson, it is important that one looks into that elected official's district (map, demographics) and their policy positions (legislative committee assignments, legislation introduced, and legislation passed). All of this information can be found on the elected official's website. Therefore, an internship with Congressman Juan Vargas would expose one to a lot of things from constituent relations to policy-making, and even the ceremonial events that Congresspeople are invited to like the Otay Mesa East Port of Entry groundbreaking. Ultimately exposing one to the San Diego local politics network and at capital hill, which can then assist one with one's future professional endeavors. In the world of politics, government, or public service, who one works for and who one knows are very important for one's professional growth and opportunities.

Option 3: Opportunities with the Local Government:

Furthermore, another example with the City of San Diego in relation to US-Mexico relations, politics in Mexico, or Latin American relations at large would be interning with the *Mayor's Office of Global Affairs* or with the *City's Office of Immigrant Affairs*. These types of local offices can be found across the country, especially in major cities like Los Angeles, Chicago, Atlanta, New York, etc. And sometimes these two topics of global and immigrant affairs are combined under one office. But to expand on the internship opportunities at the local level and how these opportunities can impact one's future, especially for someone interested in US-Mexico relations, politics in Mexico, and Latin American relations at large, working with a local government like the City of San Diego, would similarly expose one to a network of individuals who work in what is described to be "subnational diplomacy" or local level international relations.

The City of San Diego is the largest border city of the United States, and maintains a strong relationship with Mexico, the Mexican state of Baja California, and the City of Tijuana, especially when it comes to issues that impact or involve both sides of the border: transportation and mobility, environmental concerns (air quality, the Tijuana River Valley, the oceans), tourism and the economy, and immigration. Therefore, an internship with either offices would provide an intern with the experience, exposure, information, and network pertaining to the US-Mexico issues, but at a local level that then can be utilized to obtain a job in any other capacity involving these specific issues.

What does an entry level job look like for someone who completed this internship? Take, for example, a position such as the Protocol Manager or Community Representative at the local level. The Protocol Manager is the staffer that works for the Mayor's Office of Global Affairs and its most likely tasked with assisting the Director of Global Affairs with any and all tasks needed, advise the Mayor on proper greeting procedures, etiquette prior to meeting with foreign dignitaries, writing the informational memos for the Mayor to prepare them on all of the relevant information relating to the foreign dignitaries and the states where they are from, and attending international/binational events with or on behalf of the Mayor. Another common example is that of a Community Representative, also known as a Field Representative with an elected official (i.e. Mayor, Councilmember, State Assemlymember, State Senator, Congressperson, or U.S. Senator). In this role, one can be tasked with handling community relations and constituent services, essentially connecting the community with City Hall resources and attending events alongside the elected official or on behalf of the elected official. These entry level roles would be the next step for an intern interested in the issues previously described to begin their careers within the field of international relations, at a local level, and mostly working on US-Mexico issues. Again, this would all depend on the intern's performance, interests, and network.

Option 4: Opportunities in the Private Sector:

A fourth and final example of an internship involving US-Mexico relations, politics in Mexico, and Latin American relations at large within San Diego would be within the private sector with an organization like the *San Diego Regional Chamber of Commerce* (The Chamber), which is a nonprofit organization designed to bring together businesses, conduct policy research, and host events to advance San Diego's economy regionally. This organization is highly involved with the many public service organizations in the region from San Diego City Council, the Mayor's Office, the County of San Diego Board of Supervisors, the California State legislature, the San Diego Congressional Delegation, the San Diego Association of Governments, the many mayors and city councils across the region, and with the public and private sectors of Tijuana, Baja California, and Mexico at large. They host regular trips to Mexico City, Washington D.C., and Sacramento to advance the San Diego region's goals and agenda while also requesting for resources that will make San Diego the best place to work and live.

This is an organization that also offers internships involving the following topics: external affairs, international business affairs, and events & marketing. To continue with the previous example of a student interested in US-Mexico relations, the external affairs and/or international business affairs internships would be the most adequate. The external affairs internship consists of assisting the public affairs and policy research team on conducting research on the many policy areas (i.e. housing and land use, public health, veteran affairs, small businesses, environment, child care and education) offering advice to other organizations or legislative bodies. While this internship topic does not directly involve political issues, it still allows one to work on these policy topics with a regional focus here in the San Diego-Tijuana region, also known as the CaliBaja region or "La Mega Region."

The Chamber is also involved in many of the binational events given that it is a regional chamber of commerce; events like the groundbreaking of the Otay Mesa East Port of Entry, which was mentioned previously, but not explained. The Otay

Mesa East Port of Entry is a project at the US-Mexico border between both countries to create a third port of entry. This third port of entry will not only help with reducing the wait times at the border, but also address the poor air quality at the San Diego-Tijuana border region. Events involving the Otay Mesa East Port of Entry, are events where many elected officials and leaders from the regional, state, and even federal governments will attend, meaning a great opportunity to network.

Lastly, the international business affairs (IB affairs) internship would consist of working closely with the IB affairs team promoting regional businesses, analyzing business decisions that impact the region, and working closely to assist policy makers on both sides of the border to pass legislation that will assist businesses in San Diego and Tijuana. While this role has a more economic, business concentration it still exposes an intern to this regional network of business and government leaders. Additionally, the IB affairs team at the Chamber works closely with other organizations like the San Diego World Trade Center, the Tijuana Economic Development Corporation, the San Diego Regional Economic Development Corp, and many other international businesses based out of the San Diego region. Overall, working with the Chamber would allow for one to create and navigate a network both with the public sector and private sectors, meaning more opportunities for one's future.

How Do I Build My Network? Take Care to Develop a Relationship with Everyone at the Workplace.

A professional network can be described as being the group of people that focuses on interactions and relationships for professional growth, new opportunities, and development. This can be established by creating connections and contacts within the field. Typically by attending events, conferences, meetings, and being introduced to already established networks. How can one obtain access to already established networks? Through internships.

Internships programs that are considered to be strong programs not only train and teach their interns, but introduce them to a network of professionals. Therefore, it is vital that while one is on the search for the "perfect" internship, one takes into consideration the amount of exposure to an established network of professionals. It is through these networks that one can obtain a full time job after completion of their internship and studies. As previously stated, in the field of government, politics, and international relations, who one knows is KEY. Who one knows is key for two reasons. First, it is often through these networks that one is offered a job. In some cases, it is the younger professionals who assist the next generations with job offers and take them under their wings. Second, who you work for or intern with is also important. While some interns obtain employment with the organization they intern with, others do not. Instead some obtain employment with other organizations because of the networking they did during their time as interns. These job offers can be offered by the other professionals inside the network, and others within the network can also speak positively of one and support one through recommendations. Again, who one knows is KEY. Some recommendations might carry "special" weight, which can benefit one when it comes to job procurement.

What does a successful intern that also succeeds in networking look like? This is an intern that obtains an internship with an organization that is well connected and known within the field. This intern also decides to work for an alumni of their university, which is not necessary, but a great advantage in the process of job procurement. Job procurement is afterall one of the most important reasons to do an internship, in addition to transferring the skills learned. This intern would then demonstrate commitment and great interest to their assignments, ask a lot of good questions, actively engage with other interns and staff, and demonstrate critical thinking skills. This intern would attend as many networking opportunities, share their story: who they are, where they study, and what their ambitions are.

In an ideal world, the intern described would be offered either an extension to their internship or a part time position, with intentions to then offer a full time job. With this extension, this intern will continue to gain experience, demonstrate longevity and commitment to an organization, and can continue to network. With time and networking with the same individuals and new individuals within the field, this intern will slowly become a part of this network, building a "brand" for themselves. Soon after, the intern can be offered full time positions from members of the network or in the event that the intern becomes tired of being an intern or believes they are ready for a full time position, they can contact members of the network expressing interest in their organizations. It is most likely the case that the intern will seek positions that are similar to their roles as interns where they can showcase their skills and transfer the skills learned. Once the intern expresses interest with multiple members of the network, this intern will most likely receive multiple offers and will begin to do interviews, and will have to begin negotiations of items such as salary and the type of work one is expected to do. At the end of this process, this intern selects the job that they find to be the most beneficial to them, and they believe will allow them to continue building their network, develop professionally, and succeed as a young professional.

Find a mentor.

Additionally, it is ideal that the network that this intern became involved with and helped them get a full time job was also a network with mentors – and most importantly that assisted in the procurement of a job with an office of mentors as well. One needs the support of their colleagues and superiors to continue learning about the field, the subject matter, and profession in order to become a successful professional who can then do the same for the next generations of professionals. These professional networks are a never ending cycle of older professionals mentoring young professionals, and showing them how these systems work and how one can apply one's studies and degrees to the real world.

Longevity is critical.

What does an intern that fails to succeed in networking look like? Some individuals opt out to become involved with a plethora of organizations and numerous short term internships. While this can result in a diversified portfolio and background, it does not always assist one in establishing oneself within a strong network of professionals. Longevity, commitment, and loyalty to one organization can be viewed as a great thing for someone. This demonstrates that one is committed to working to advance the goals of an organization, can work effectively with a group of people, and has loyalty. Loyalty is another vital factor within the field of government and public service, especially when working for an elected official. Elected officials need to know that you are loyal to them, that one can be trusted to advance their agenda, and that one is passionate about the policy priorities that the elected has. Some would argue that working for an elected person is a privilege, therefore, when one is presented with the opportunity one must take it very seriously. But to return back to the intern that fails to succeed in networking as a result of participating in a plethora of internships, this can then add a layer of difficulty when procuring a full time job after one completes their studies. Employers can also interpret the plethora of internships as being an individual that lacks the skills or assets to work with a team and/or organization. It presents the questions of why one has not been able to stay with an organization for more than three months or how one can hire someone who has not been in a role for more than three months?

Why Should I Build a Digital Network As Well?:

Establishing and maintaining a network is of high importance for one's future, and the same can be said about a digital network. To be more specific, this digital network is created and managed through the social media platform known as LinkedIn. This is an app designed for business and professional development that was launched in the early 2000s, but that in recent times has become a staple in career development. How exactly does this platform work or how can one grow their network with this app? LinkedIn is an app much like the other social media platforms where one has to create an account, and create a brand for oneself. This is a platform beyond a digital resume, it's a platform where one can create a detailed biography describing one's experience and future aspirations, where one can share their professional achievements, where one can perform job searches, and apply for jobs. It essentially is a one stop shop for professionals to conduct all matters related to their growth and development.

More specifically, a strong LinkedIn account has the following attributes. First, a professional headshot that can be used in public forums to showcase who you are as a professional. Essentially a headshot that can be used to put on flyers or at conferences. Second, a bio section that accurately describes your most recent occupation and organization that you work for. This is a section where students can list where and what they are studying. Third, an "about" section that includes your elevator pitch of who you are, who you work for, what you do, and your future goals. Fourth, an "experience" section with an updated digital resume, listing all of your relevant experiences with a detailed description of what those roles entailed to get a sense of your expertise, knowledge, and laborious experiences. Fifth, an updated and detailed "education" section. In this section it is imperative that one include the relevant courses that one has taken to showcase one's areas of interests or area of focus. This is important because in most cases one seeks jobs and a career path in the area of focus and interest that one pursued as a student. Additionally, since a young professional lacks the experience, it is one's expertise that is of much importance to an employer. Sixth, on LinkedIn, one should be posting about one's acceptance to a new position, the completion of an internship, the completion of a certification program, one's graduation, essentially any milestones that impact one's career and future as a professional. It is important to build one's network by "connecting" with other relevant professionals that one meets in person at events. This way one can engage with their posts, and also receive announcements of new jobs and opportunities that will further assist in excelling professionally. Much like the in-person network, this group of individuals, through this platform, are to be utilized to further advance one's professional goals.

Conclusion

Ultimately, one must ensure that they search for an internship that is interesting, that will provide one with new skills, will force one to think critically, prepare one for a full time job in the specific field, and that will introduce one to a solidified network of professionals who can help one to continue growing and developing professionally. Furthermore, there are a plethora of internships with different goals and outcomes within a topic alone, meaning that there is something for everyone, it just requires one to do extensive research. One must also have an understanding of what one's interests are, what types of roles one is interested in, and where one wants to work after the completion of their studies. This decision, just like deciding which university one attends, is very important to one's professional future. One must be willing to step out of one's comfort zone to ask questions, participate in the internship in a strategic manner, and maximize the accessibility to the network of professionals by joining one's supervisor to events, conferences, and meetings; and engaging with the professionals to get to know them. At the end of the day who one knows, who one works for, where one studies, who one becomes, and who one mentors are all very important factors that will dictate one's professional career, reputation, and overarching future. Lastly, when working in government one is always being watched by the people one serves, others who want one's job, or by future employers, therefore, every decision should be strategic and meaningful.

II
DOING PUBLIC POLICY: OBTAINING AN INTERNSHIP IN THE PUBLIC SECTOR
Amanda Mueller

Roadmap:

Key Takeaways:
- The public sector includes organizations owned, controlled, and managed by the local, state, or federal government.
- When looking for a public sector internship, consider your interests, skills, and future career aspirations.
- Be wary of personality quizzes that dictate what career you should choose!

"As the youngest on the team and the only woman, I had to work incredibly hard during the first few months to prove myself and receive the respect I deserve...this internship has given me the tools and experience to deal with intolerance, and empowered me to be more confident and assertive in my interactions."

What is the Public Sector?

Public sector organizations are owned, controlled, and managed by the government or other state-run bodies. This includes all government agencies at the local, state, and federal levels. In the public sector, jobs are typically funded by taxes rather than revenue. Some examples include working for a congressperson or local government official, the county, or for the federal government. Conversely, private sector organizations are owned, controlled and managed by individuals, groups or business entities.

Tips on Finding an Internship in the Public Sector

Think About What Interests You

Begin by asking yourself: what interests me? In order to get the most out of the internship, I would recommend choosing a field or topic that interests you. Things to consider: What subjects do you like at school? What job would you like to do? What do you see yourself doing long term? What work-life balance are you looking for? Other things that helped me were taking a variety of classes within my political science major, to help find topics that I was interested in. I have gravitated toward security-focused issues like transnational crime, which in turn got me interested in the way these criminals are caught and prosecuted. For example, I was interested in learning more about law enforcement, so I prioritized being proactive and persistent in my internship with the Sheriff's Department. I originally thought that I was only qualified for an administrative assistant position, although that kind of work does not interest me. Ultimately, I was asked to work in technology and communications, which I found a lot more captivating. Part of the reason I love studying international relations is because it is a constantly changing field with many moving parts. Working with technology is similar because there are constantly new discoveries made and new information to process. I found that it's exciting to learn new things and figure out challenging problems. This internship even aligned with classes I took during my time as an undergraduate student, mostly involving American politics and the judicial system. The graduate class that aligned the most with my internship would be my course on global policing. To be more specific, in this course we discussed jurisdiction, and as an intern for the Sheriff's Department I also have to pay close attention to jurisdiction, and which agencies have access to different frequencies and channels. This is important for security purposes, to limit the spread of information, but also for efficiency so government officials and emergency personnel do not have to wade through irrelevant information.

Think About Your Skills

There are countless personality and compatibility tests online, with varying degrees of seriousness. On websites like Buzzfeed, you can learn what kind of bread you are (I am banana bread). The Myers-Briggs personality test, which is rather well known, divides people into sixteen different categories based on pairs of dichotomous variables: extroversion and inversion, intuition and sensing, thinking and feeling, and judging and perceiving. Based on your combination, you can get lists of strengths and weaknesses, romantic compatibility with other combinations, and recommendations for careers. This sounds like great information, but this test is actually very controversial. Critics have labeled it as inconsistent, not being based on empirical psychology, and forcing people who experience and feel things on a spectrum into strict binaries. When I took the test and received the category of INFJ (Introvert, Intuition, Feeling, Judging) it gave me career recommendations of teaching, social work, therapy, and healthcare. While these are excellent professions made up of talented people, these are not things I am interested in or skilled at. To indicate success in many jobs in Political Science or International Relations, I would have had to receive the Extroverted, Intuition, Thinking, Judging (ENTJ) combination.

Another controversial personality test is the Enneagram. This test separates people into three categories (emotional, intellectual, and instinctual intelligence) with three subtypes within these categories for nine possible types. When I took this test, I was placed in the category of nine or the peacemaker. Jobs recommended for Enneagram nines include teachers, artists, and counselors. In order to be recommended for jobs that fit my interests and studies, I would have had to score a one, a six, or an eight. Although personality quizzes can be fun, I do not recommend taking the results too seriously or making any major life decisions based on them.

One personality test that I actually found useful in thinking about my skills was the Clifton Strengths Assessment. Instead of sorting people into categories, it instead gives you a list of five strengths out of thirty-four total. Some examples include responsibility, positivity, focus, and communication. It also gives you in depth information about these strengths and ways to apply them. I found that this test had a lot more flexibility and nuance, and encapsulated how I perceive myself in an organized and effective way. I took this test when I was working as a student mentor at the University of San Diego, and I applied my strengths of empathy, harmony, and consistency into this role. I was helping first year students transition to college life, and I found myself navigating through their feelings of vulnerability and uncertainty. Within my internship at the Sheriff's department, I heavily relied on my strength of input, or accumulating and organizing information. Part of my job is to take raw data from different organizations, and compile it into a spreadsheet to make it easier to read. Therefore, being able to spot both patterns and mistakes is essential.

Think About Where You Might Want to Work in the Future

I ultimately chose to get an internship in the public sector because I knew that I wanted to work in the public sector in the future. Working for the County of San Diego as a student intern felt more manageable than jumping straight into a federal government job after I graduate. This set me up for success in several different ways. First, having such a detailed and invasive background check will look good on future endeavors. I have already proven that I have a clean record, and that I can withstand such a deep dive into my history. Second, due to the nature of the information stored on the radios and the communication that goes on over them, I have security clearance. This is good practice for dealing with sensitive and confidential information in the future, as well as proving to future employers that I can keep information confidential.

Third, this internship gave me a clear picture on working in a law enforcement environment. The culture at the Sheriff's Department is still very male-dominated and relies heavily on traditional gender roles. As the youngest on the team and the only woman, I had to work incredibly hard during the first few months to prove myself and receive the respect I deserved. When I interviewed a female retired FBI agent for this course, she mentioned that her greatest accomplishment in her 20+ years of service was being able to succeed at her job despite being a woman in a leadership position and having to rise above harassment, ridicule, and disrespect. In a similar way, this internship has given me tools and experience to deal with intolerance, and empowered me to be more confident and assertive in my interactions. I have also learned and practiced skills that are not explicitly labeled in my job description like public speaking, technical writing, and working within tight deadlines.

My Personal Experience in a Public Sector Internship

Getting an internship in this field is difficult, but not impossible. As a graduate student in the Masters of Arts in

International Relations program at the University of San Diego (USD), I was able to get an internship with the County of San Diego. When looking for an internship, I studied the website "governmentjobs.com" and focused my search on the County and City of San Diego. I located the student worker position, filled out the application, and sent in my resume. I did not have to do a proper job interview. Once accepted, I was given a list of contacts in each department that was accepting student workers, and I was instructed to contact those whose department matched up best with my field of study. As a political science and international relations student, I contacted and left voicemails for the following offices and departments at the County: the Clerk's Office, the District Attorney's Office, Library Services, Probation, Public Defender, Registrar of Voters, and the Sheriff's Department. Besides the Registrar of Voters, which I had already worked for through the USD Votes club for the 2021 gubernatorial election, the only department I heard back from was the Sheriff's Department. My contact offered me several positions, including working in the commissary at a local correctional facility or working as an administrative assistant at different sheriff stations. I accepted the administrative assistant position at the Wireless Services Division, where radios for sheriffs, emergency personnel, and other government agencies are programmed, maintained, and organized. Immediately after, I began the background process. I gave three character and career references, and I had to fill out a questionnaire with over 500 questions about my personal, family, legal, and academic history. It was invasive, but since I have security clearance and work with sensitive information, I understood why the screening process was so intense. After making sure all of this paperwork was filled out correctly, I was given a Voice Stress Analysis test, similar to a polygraph test, to determine whether my answers were truthful. After passing the Voice Stress Analysis test, I was fingerprinted and the Sheriff's Department ran a full background check on me. I passed the background check, and was cleared to start working. This entire process took a little over two months. I was contacted by Human Resources and my supervisor to discuss my pay and set my hours. My supervisor had supervised student workers before, and he was very flexible and understanding regarding my hours and the impact it could have on my academic performance.

When I arrived for my first day, I was informed that there was a greater need for a programming intern rather than an administrative assistant. I was trained to fix and program radios as well as maintain and organize the databases used to keep track of all of these radios. A typical shift includes meeting with technicians to learn programming tools and assist with current projects, performing administrative duties with online files, and working on and updating the online database. My greatest accomplishment is making the database more organized and accessible. I analyzed and updated thousands of individual assets, or radios, and lines of code to look for mistakes and make the important information stand out. I created a new system to make taking inventory of the radios faster and more efficient, and organized all of the radios being stored in our warehouse into crates based on the radios' capabilities. I hope that this will make it easier for future employees, as well the emergency personnel we serve, to communicate more effectively and accurately. I would recommend this internship as a short-term job to gain experience in a law enforcement environment. There are many different roles within this internship, including administrative assistant, programming intern, and installation mechanic. An administrative assistant actively engages with our clients, which are members of different county organizations, and can help permanent staff with everything from accounting to scheduling. An installation mechanic takes the programmed radios and installs them into cars, motorcycles, helicopters, etc. As interns, we work in harmony with the permanent staff to keep things running smoothly. Overall, I think this would be a good fit for people with multiple skills or areas of interest.

Another Perspective: Sabrina Richards on Interning for Congressman Darrell Issa

To get another perspective, I interviewed my classmate Sabrina on her time as an intern for a congressman:

Q: What drew you to an internship in the public sector?
A: "I wanted to pursue an internship in the public sector because I hope to eventually serve our country as an elected official. I wanted to dip my toes into it to see what it is like. I was unsure if I wanted to go straight into politics or go to law school first, and this internship helped me learn that you really need a foundational career before you can make the jump into politics, and that was valuable knowledge to gain since I wanted to make an informed decision about going to law school."

Q: What was your experience like?
A: "The experience was great! Everyone in the office was so welcoming and I learned a great deal about how a federal office works. A large part of my job was responding to calls, voicemails, and emails from constituents in the Congressman's district. In addition, I completed casework, meaning when a constituent needed help from the Congressman, I would act on the office's behalf to other government agencies and help the constituent get pointed in the right direction. A lot of this work involved helping constituents dealing with long waits times with the United States Citizenship and Immigration Services."

Q: *Do you have any advice for students looking for internships in the public sector?*
A: "I would encourage students looking to work in the public sector to apply to a lot of different offices! I applied to intern for a number of different Congresspeople, even in other states, and was excited for whatever opportunity presented itself!"

Conclusion

Overall, a public sector internship is an excellent choice for those interested in working for the government. In my experience, the fast-paced environment and countless learning opportunities far outweigh the intense application process. After finishing this graduate program and leaving my student internship, I plan to take the Foreign Service exam and begin the federal application processes for the FBI and CIA. I believe that my experience in the public sector has given me a major advantage for these future endeavors!

III

POLITICS & THE PRIVATE SECTOR: OBTAINING AN INTERNSHIP IN THE PRIVATE SECTOR
Ryan Haile

Roadmap:
i.	Why is this Important? School and Life are Very Different Beasts
ii.	How to Increase One's Internship Prospects
iii.	Recommended Internship Steps and Options in the Private Sector Related to International Relations
iv.	My Personal International Relations Internship Experience

Key Takeaways:
- The search for an internship starts long before the actual "search."
- The rigors of life far surpass the rigors of school.
- A lack of work experience while one is in school is detrimental to long-term success.
- Developing relationships with professors and other professionals is vital to obtaining an internship.

"Developing relationships with professors and other professionals is vital to obtaining an internship."

Introduction

No matter what career path an individual is pursuing, the ultimate question remains the same: what steps during one's educational career are the most conducive to obtaining a quality job after finishing school? A question that students should be asking themselves is "what can I do during my education to ensure I am ready for post-graduate life?" There are a host of items that a student must accomplish to ensure that she has the maximum amount of job opportunities as possible upon obtaining their degree. These items include earning quality grades, maintaining a sterling reputation regarding character and work ethic, developing relationships with faculty and other university staff who will be willing to provide him or her with letters of recommendation, racking up an extensive civil and community service record by participating in local community outreach programs, staying out of legal and school disciplinary trouble, and, last but not least, obtaining work experience, including, but not limited to, quality internships in the field that the student ultimately desires to work in. That is a long checklist .

This chapter will focus on the search for an internship: how does one find potential internship positions, and what steps should a student take to acquire such an internship? Part I of this chapter primarily explains a potential path to obtaining an international relations internship in the private sector. Part A will explain why obtaining an internship in one's desired career field is vital to maximizing potential opportunities following the completion of school. Part B will explain what a student can do as part of her schooling to make her more attractive to potential internship employers, and how to maximize her chances of obtaining the best possible internship that she desires. Part C will discuss several effective practices for finding internship opportunities, as well as describe several potential internship types in the private sector that relate to international relations. In Part D, I will describe my personal experience of how I received an internship involving international relations in the private sector, and the positive impact it has had on my future career aspirations by presenting me with a potential long-term job opportunity.

Why Is This Important? School and Life Are Very Different Beasts.

The rigors experienced during employment are far different than those that are characteristic of the educational experience. There is usually far less discretion in missing one's designated work assignments than there is to missing class. Additionally, there is usually less flexibility in choosing one's hours. In school, one usually has some discretion in picking one's schedule, and structuring one's schedule in alignment with one's personal preferences and lifestyle. In contrast, the hours that one works in a job are usually assigned primarily based on what the employer needs. Further, in the workplace, one is apt to receive more constructive criticism than one (typically) receives in school. Teachers are normally trained to treat students a bit more softly. This is not the case in the workplace; an employer has to deliver results, and as such, will be less hesitant to deliver criticism than many teachers would be. In addition, this is a function of working people needing to deliver results both to keep their jobs and to potentially receive promotions to better positions. Finally, in the workplace, a single worker is usually just one part of a larger team (i.e., one individual part of a whole machine). Consequently, an employee is depended upon by her fellow employees and supervisor to get her job done so that the entire job gets done. As such, valuable teamwork skills are built in the process of getting work experience that simply is not quite the same in the educational process.

A lack of work experience is detrimental to success.

The above analysis suggests that obtaining some work experience during one's college or graduate school years is essential in order to maximize their long-term work opportunities. A lack of work experience will do nothing to show prospective employers that a new graduate is ready to transition from the life of a student to that of a full-time employee. With international relations in particular, the issues pertain to real-world, dire situations that affect not only one country, but the entire world. As such, it is vital that a student rack up as much work experience as possible while in school (whether one works only during the summer, or also during the school year, depends on the schedules and capacity of individual students). One way that a student can obtain this work experience and yet still engage in a field relevant to their ultimate career goal (which, since you are reading this book, we are assuming is international relations), is to obtain an internship that both provides the valuable tangible work skills listed above, as well as developing the particular skills necessary to achieving her ultimate career goal.

So now you want the internship. What do you have to do to get it?

Consequently, if one wants to work in the field of international relations long term, a strong academic record, and substantial community service participation will likely have a minimal impact on one's ultimate career path when compared to obtaining working experience in the field that one desires to ultimately have a career. In the field of international relations, this work experience is particularly valuable because it allows the students to develop the work ethic and skills that many say are necessary to develop in order to obtain the best internship possible. Additionally, participating in an internship that involves international relations issues will give students an opportunity to apply some of the theories and principles that they learn in some of their classes to real-world international relations' issues. This practical experience is vital for a student to develop into a well-rounded job candidate that private firms working in the field of international relations would want to hire.

If a student takes the advice and information laid out in the following subsections of Part I, then this student is highly likely to be well prepared to hit the ground running on their internship search. This will put the student in an excellent position for purposes of landing a job in the ultimate career path in which they want to work in international relations.

How to Increase One's Internship Prospects

Obtaining an internship in international relations can at times be difficult; there are only so many internships to go around, with a large number of students duking it out to obtain the most attractive positions. As such, it is important that students take advantage of every opportunity to pad their resumes and ensure that their qualifications are top notch to remain competitive candidates for these highly sought-after positions. While any prior work experience will obviously be a factor, most students will likely lack much prior work experience considering their young age and status as students. Consequently, the best way that students can enhance their attractiveness to prospective internship employers is through school. A student can do this in a number of ways:

- Achieving good grades
- Participating in extracurricular activities, particularly extracurricular activities that relate to the field of international relations, such as Model United Nations
- Engaging in community service
- Participating in student government
- Taking classes that teach useful skills such as proficiency in Microsoft Excel or Word
- Developing quality relationships with teachers in order to be in a position to request letters of recommendation

The most important part of the internship search process actually begins before you go out actually looking for internship positions, and that is developing as many qualifications as possible and the best record possible.

As one might expect, achieving quality grades is very important to maximizing the number of internship opportunities a student can possibly obtain. Prospective internship employers want to see that potential interns have developed a work ethic and level of perseverance that is necessary to being able to effectively contribute to the employer's organization, and one of the main ways that an employer can gauge this is by examining the grades that prospective interns achieve. Grades are an easy metric for employers to utilize to compare prospective interns. As such, students should do everything they can to get as high of grades as possible.

But what if your grades are not great?

However, if a student's grades are not quite where they would like them to be, that student need not despair. They can make up for slightly below-par grades by enhancing her school achievements in other areas. One important possibility is participation in school organizations, particularly one such as political organizations, professional fraternities, or speech and debate caucuses. Such an experience will show a prospective employer that students are able to work with others and will also confer valuable skills that are tied to the field of international relations, which could enhance a student's attractiveness for purposes of obtaining an internship. Students should try to obtain leadership posts in these school organizations because this will demonstrate initiative and moxie to prospective employers, as well as demonstrating effective leadership skills.

Developing skills in important applications such as Microsoft Excel and Word can go a long way towards differentiating oneself from other internship applicants. Such applications are often vital to one's responsibilities in the workplace. A student's ability to achieve proficiency in these skills prior to applying for internship opportunities will show prospective employers that she is ready to contribute and add value to the employee's organization immediately, and also save the employer from having to train the student in these applications himself.

Finally, and perhaps even most importantly, students should develop individual relationships with professors and other school faculty. One way to do this is to attend school events where faculty are present. Another way is to regularly attend teacher office hours and communicate with teachers by email regularly. This will enable these students both to ask these professors for letters of recommendation and will also encourage these professors to impart potential internship opportunities to students. The value of professors passing along internship opportunities to students cannot be overstated; these professors likely have contacts in the field of international relations, and recommendations from school professors is likely one of the most common ways that many students obtain an internship. A prospective employer will want to hear from neutral third parties why a particular student is a good fit for a particular internship position, and letters of recommendation are an excellent medium for imparting that information.

One final note: although it is not absolutely essential, one other activity that a student can participate in while in school that will likely enhance her internship prospects is to study abroad. This will give a student valuable international experience, which obviously can be an important factor in obtaining an internship in the field of international relations. Such experience will demonstrate to an employer that a student truly wants to be involved in international relations long term, which could help a student to differentiate herself from other potential internship applicants.

Recommended Internship Steps and Options in the Private Sector Related to International Relations

There are a number of pragmatic steps a student who wishes to obtain a private sector internship related to international relations should take. These steps include exhaustive research to find private companies that contain an international component to their business, contacting the representatives of companies that a student might wish to intern for, exhaustively utilizing one's own personal contacts for potential internship options.

Step 1: Search out all the opportunities.

The first step that a student should take is to perform an exhaustive search for private companies whose businesses relate in some way to international relations. One common way to do this is simply to research multinational corporations on the internet and see which of these corporations have business operations that include a nexus with some international component. One should start by googling international corporations. Once a student finds a list of some international corporations, they should look to see which of these corporations are involved in an area that interests them. A lot of these firms will be firms that engage in importing and exporting products in and out of the country because such a business model necessitates compliance with international regimes and laws. Thus, these companies are likely to have compliance departments and government affairs teams that deal with issues relating to international government actions, and analyzing international laws.

Step 2: Apply and apply and apply!

Once a student finds a list of private companies relating to international relations that they have interest in interning for, they need to start contacting the representatives of those companies or search through their information to see how to go about applying for an internship. It would be a good idea to contact a lot of different companies and send out many different applications because these internship opportunities are often very competitive, and it would be beneficial to have as many options as possible. Be persistent! If you get radio silence the first time, then try again! A student should make sure that when they apply for an internship, they follow all the instructions promulgated by the companies as part of their application process, and include all relevant information and documents required by the application.

Step 3: Seek out personal contacts to help.

It is very important that a student utilize their own personal contacts to identify potential opportunities. One of the most common ways to get a job or internship is through such personal contacts. As many often say, "it is not what you know" that gets you a particular opportunity, but rather "who you know" that ends up doing the trick. This is because people a student knows that is offering an internship will likely have a greater interest in seeing the student succeed than random strangers, and so may choose them over other potential applicants for a position, all things being equal. Additionally, it would not be a bad idea for a student to utilize the career counseling office at their school. Oftentimes, these career counseling offices know of a significant amount of potential internship opportunities, and a student can meet with a counselor to ask which of those opportunities potentially relate to international relations. A lot of times, career counseling goes underused, so take advantage!

Several potential private sector options for internships that may relate to international relations are multinational corporations, international law firms, relevant think tanks, and NGOs that deal with international issues such as human trafficking and climate change. As previously stated, multinational corporations often conduct business in multiple countries, and as such, contain departments that have interactions with governmental and legal authorities in such countries. International law firms would involve activities related to international relations by the very virtue of needing to understand the laws of foreign countries as the source of their business. Think tanks often focus on global and geopolitical issues, which by their very definition relate to international relations. For example, the Center for Strategic and International Studies (CSIS), "is a bipartisan, nonprofit policy research organization & think take dedicated to advancing practical ideas to address the world's greatest challenges" (https://www.csis.org/about). All of these types of private sector organizations would very likely include internship opportunities that relate to international relations.

My Personal International Relations Internship Experience

I was incredibly fortunate to be able to obtain a fantastic internship in the private sector that was heavily tied to international relations. I was offered a position as an Analyst in Qualcomm's Government Affairs team. Qualcomm is a massive multi-national corporation (MNC), and as such, has heavy ties to a variety of countries and a robust international presence. Consequently, it is important for Qualcomm to stay abreast of legal and regulatory requirements in a number of different countries for purposes of ensuring compliance with applicable labor and trade and export requirements. Qualcomm maintains a significant lobbying and government relations team to affect this purpose, and that team is called Government Affairs.

I found the opportunity through a heavy process of networking. In my search process, I left no stone unturned. I looked on every company's website that I could find for potential internship opportunities. I went to all of my professors to inquire as to whether any of them knew of any opportunities. However, the way I obtained my internship was actually by taking advantage of my personal network; I reached out to every personal contact that I knew, and eventually one of my personal contacts connected me with someone who worked on Qualcomm's Government Affairs team, and I was able to secure an interview. After receiving an interview, the hard work I had done during my schooling gave me a leg up on other candidates for the position, as I had sterling grades, numerous letters of recommendation, significant extracurricular experience, and had traveled abroad.

The experience I had interning for Qualcomm was truly life-changing because it truly showed me that a career in international relations was something I needed to have. I learned many effective skills, including how to analyze laws and regulations in different countries, and how to aid corporate executives in managing long-term corporate strategies in an increasingly interdependent world. In addition, I was able to learn how to add value to my organization, and how to make myself useful at every turn, which has proven incredibly valuable to my long-term career prospects. I also learned how to work as part of a team that is involved in international relations' activities, and this has enhanced my attractiveness to prospective long-term employers after I graduate. In fact, I have been offered a follow up internship at Qualcomm next summer. The position I was offered is in Qualcomm's trade and export compliance organization and is an even more senior position than I had during my experience at Government Affairs. It also could potentially lead to a full-time position. Thus, my internship experience has gone a long way toward setting me up to obtaining a long-term career in the international relations field after I graduate.

Conclusion

Getting an internship is never easy, and oftentimes the hardest part is the search process. The search process, however, can be made easy if one builds as impressive of a resume as possible while in school. Obtaining an internship is incredibly important for preparing a student for life after school. One can increase their internship prospects in a number of ways, including obtaining good grades and compiling an impressive community service record. There are a number of steps a student should take when searching for an internship in the private sector in international relations, including comprehensively searching out all private sector opportunities. My own personal internship in Qualcomm's Government Affairs division truly changed my life. While obtaining an internship is always hard, it is also always worth it!

PART TWO

The Keys to Success

IV
HOW TO BE A SUCCESSFUL INTERN: ADVICE FOR PERFORMING AT YOUR BEST
Sabrina Richards

Roadmap:

Key Takeaways:
- This chapter will take you door-to-door in your internship, from the minute you walk into the interview, to when you say goodbye to everyone on your last day.
- I will walk through tips for success at each stage of your internship to help challenge you to impress your employer!

"As the internship provides multiple resources and opportunities, the key to any successful internship is what the intern brings to the table."

Introduction

Higher education is about more than just academics. A lot of the time, it is the experiences that college students have outside of the classroom that have the most impact. As students embark on the pathway to higher education, there are many opportunities available at colleges that are most critical for learning. Experiences may include apprenticeships, coursework, athletics, and work study programs to name a few. One of the most important of these is the art and science behind being a successful intern. After participating in various internships during these past few years, I believe all students should actively participate in at least one internship during their college experience. This internship experience will allow for gaining all types of insight, knowledge, and job-related skills. An internship provides access to real experiences and the ability to be hands-on in a career path that you may choose. Therefore, make sure you select one that will provide knowledge, experience, and networking opportunities. Since you are reading this book, I am assuming you are looking for an internship in the international relations or political science field.

Here's the key: As the internship provides multiple resources and opportunities, the key to any successful internship is *what the intern brings to the table.*

Seeking out job opportunities is sometimes a full-time job itself, and this is true of an internship. Being successful as an intern starts long before applying for an internship. It is important to tailor your social media profile to truly illustrate who you are. Use a professional image and build a LinkedIn account, post your resume, letters of recommendations from faculty or previous employers, and academic interests (make sure to look at the in-depth process analysis in this book). It is critical to ensure any other social media accounts you may have are professional and appropriate. Treat the search process like you would if you were searching for a full-time position (sometimes, an internship, especially paid, can be). Ensuring the right internship will take time and dedication but the rewards will be enormous.

Be Dedicated, Perseverant, and Organized.

So assuming you have read this far in the book and not just my above summary, you have already learned how to look for the right internships, nail the interview, and become selected for the opportunity.

What do you do once you have secured the internship?
Be a successful intern.
Here's why.

Being a successful intern is important because a lot of times, organizations will look to their interns first when there is a position to be filled. Organizations hire interns knowing that they may become their next staff member. Organizations want to only train employees once and if they can hire a valuable intern they are then getting more bang for their buck as they could potentially offer the intern a full time position when the internship is completed. As the company invests in the intern, it is critical that the intern invests in the company. With that, a good intern does their homework before they start. Intern at a place that you could realistically get a job at. Realistically meaning within a reasonable amount of time and that you have proper qualifications.

The basis of the rest of my chapter will be based on my experience as an intern in the summer of 2022. I interned for a Congressman in San Diego. I want a career in politics and because I did my homework, I knew the importance of gaining experience in local, state, and federal politics would benefit me as I continue my career path.

There are critical areas of responsibility that are necessary for their success. The University of California at Berkeley career center boils internship success down to four key tasks for the intern: Be easy to work with, communicate clearly and kindly, learn workplace culture and norms, and leave on a good note.

Always Dress for Success.

As it is critical to dress appropriately, a college student may be concerned they do not have the proper attire for their internship. It is vital to dress not for the position you have, but for the position you want to have. Attire is important. And more so, attire does not have to be expensive to be impressive and is available for most stores. Universities tend to even host professional clothes drives where donations are collected for students to pick up or buy at a discounted process.

Typically, the organization will provide dress code guidelines when they offer an intern the position, but always dress one tier better than the company suggests. For example, if they provide golf shirts, wear a blazer or cardigan sweater over the golf shirt. Show professionalism while adhering to the standard dress. Because the office I worked in was a Congressional district office and not on Capitol Hill, the dress was more business casual. I strove to wear a business professional everyday to demonstrate I was serious about the work I was doing and would only occasionally wear jeans on Fridays with the office golf shirt.

Additionally, as you want to be available to every employee at all times, wear comfortable but appropriate shoes to the internship. If they see an intern who is fast moving they will appreciate their dedication and drive to get the work done. You do not want to be five steps behind because you did not break in your dress shoes or chose to wear stilettos. Even though ripped jeans are currently a fashion trend, do not wear ripped jeans on casual Fridays as they are considered inappropriate and unprofessional. Additionally, if you are working at a computer, do not use ear buds to play music. Wearing ear buds tells others that something else is more worthy of your attention than your coworkers, and odds are your boss will just move on to the next available intern and give them the big project. Make yourself accessible and approachable to the staff.

You Aren't In, Just Yet.

Be early on the first day of your internship. If you are on time, you are late. And never be late...any day of the internship. First impressions are lasting and more importantly, being punctual not only shows you are responsible. but also provides opportunities. An example of this if you are always on time, you will see the entire team and their capacity within the organization. If the front desk receptionist is continuously tardy, you may be able to help out. I remember always being early the first few days so I was able to sit at the big desk in the front of the office. Where you sit should not affect your productivity at the end of the day, but if you are getting the most facetime with your supervisor, it never hurts. This is a critical role as you are the first person that the patrons see when entering. Additionally, answering the early morning phone calls provides insight on who calls and what is the context of their calls. You will be able to return the voicemails left over the night before anyone else gets in, and the simple act of doing that can expand your casework or client base because when those constituents call back, they will be asking for you. All of this is knowledge that you are gaining just by being on time, being responsible, and being proactive.

As you walk in the door of your internship, remember this is an extended job interview. You earned this opportunity to prove to the organization that you are the best candidate. Odds are, you are not the only intern. When I became an intern, there were seven other interns, all male graduate or law students (I was the only woman and only undergraduate student, more on this gender dynamic later). As staffing can be a challenge for any organization, organizations have increased the number of interns they hire in hopes of finding the ideal candidate for permanent positions. For example, only one of the seven interns at the office I worked at got hired on full time.

Sometimes the organization will structure their schedule so

that interns do not even work together as they want to get the most out of each intern. An example of this is having an intern come in two days a week and having another intern come in on different days that same week. This helps the organization find the strengths in each candidate while also ensuring productivity is at maximum capacity. This is a more cut-throat method. Keep in mind a lot of the warnings I am including are for the very cut throat environments and can be applicable in foreign service or legal offices, as examples. My office was certainly more relaxed and encouraged a cooperative environment. I actually visited my old boss recently and he reminded me that I am always a part of the family.

The challenge for each intern is that they do not know their competition so one always needs to be on their A Game as they are competing against the unknown. You may know your fellow interns personally, but you usually will not know exactly what they are working on. The recommendation is to show up and be actively present with enthusiasm in all assigned tasks and when one does not have a task assigned, go find one. Never let the organization think you are lacking energy and drive. Accelerate your attitude and enthusiasm so that your productivity accelerates as well. The organization needs to believe that without you, the company will struggle with the photocopier as well as with their yearly financial plan. Learn it all and utilize all resources to learn it.

Let's be honest, you are not going to enjoy every task given to you. If you did your homework and found an internship that was exactly what you were looking for, then you probably will not have this problem. But even if you did your homework, job descriptions can be misleading. The key is, act like you love everyone. single. task. People love enthusiastic people and your boss will love seeing you so happy to be there! It's such an advantage to be a positive influence in the office.

Give 110% to Your Work!

A good intern makes the most of the work they are assigned. Do what you are asked, and then make sure to go the extra mile and include something additive to the work they produce. Interns need to learn all facets of the organization and get a good handle on the workings of the company. The organization needs to trust their interns and ensure they are capable of handling tasks, understand the importance of confidentiality, and are responsible. You do not want your boss not giving you a big project because they are unsure if you can properly handle it. An intern may be assigned general office tasks as they start the internship, but it is the intern's responsibility to prove the organization otherwise and show the leaders that one is capable of more. Simply put, be dedicated and have a passion for your work. Accepting all tasks that are given will not only make you a valuable employee it will make you a needed employee as you can pinch hit at any time. Unrelated to my Congressional internship, I also interned for the honors program at my university and an example of this occurred for me. While I was interning, I was in charge of keeping about 20 students accountable for a certain set of responsibilities and it was not always the easiest to get them to respond or be communicative. Even though I did not enjoy chasing these students down for an answer, it was a part of my job and I tried to go the extra mile to ensure everyone was informed with plenty of prior notice.

A good intern is flexible. This may sound like common sense, but it is more. A flexible attitude opens the doorway to many hidden opportunities. With the great resignation that our society is currently facing, a passionate and dedicated intern is what a company is looking for. Someone they can rely on to take on additional responsibilities if someone suddenly resigns or takes Family Medical Leave. Modern society is struggling with staffing and labor shortages so companies have recently tried to hire more interns as they can train them and provide future opportunities if they are successful. Good labor is the key to any successful business and when staff are out, customer service, production, and the bottom line all suffer. An example of this happened when I was interning was when it was the heart of summer and it seemed like everyone was out of the office. We went from seven interns to about three interns on any given day, so not only was I responsible for taking care of my own work, I had to keep up to date with my peers' casework as well to ensure there was not anything that fell through the cracks.

There Is Always the Paycheck Dilemma.

Further discussed in this book is what I like to call "the paycheck dilemma." I think it is still important to address here in relation to how a lack of paycheck can influence your work ethic. My guess is that 9 times out of 10, a valuable internship that will provide real life experience and connections will not be paid. However, once an organization hires an intern, they expect the intern to respect the rules and provide services as if they were a full time, paid employee. Although the intern may not be receiving a paycheck, the organization will expect the same dedication and drive as they would from a regular full time employee. From personal experience, I can tell you that there will be days where you question whether the amount of work you are doing is worth it to not be getting paid. It's important to push through those days to the best of your ability.

It's all about perspective. There will be a return on investment for your internship in one way or another. For me, the office was located very far from where I was staying that summer and that was also combined with an astronomical price of gas at the time. Yet, with each gallon of gas filled, I still feel like I made connections with people who will look out for me for the rest of my working career. It is near to impossible to put a price tag on that.

For the organization, hiring an intern is also an investment, regardless of the lack of the paycheck. In the business world, time is money. Training an intern takes time away from staff and their regular responsibilities as well as the intern acclimating and finding their way in the organization. An intern needs to prove they are the next best full time hire. The internship needs to be treated as if you are already hired and receiving a paycheck.

Take on a Big Project! But Don't Pull Yourself Out to Sea and Drown.

Ambition can be in all shapes and sizes. If there is a big project coming up that you know you can handle, volunteer to do it before even being asked! Make sure it is manageable though. It is not a good look if you say you can pull something off, and then for whatever reason, fall short. Specifically, oftentimes, organizations need to plan events. These events may be a professional learning day for staff, a team-builder activity, a Board of Directors meeting, an annual picnic, or even a lunch meeting with an important potential partner. As an intern, this is the best way to show you are available and anxious to handle any task. Volunteering to plan an event shows initiative and maturity because it will take planning, organizing details, contacting organizations, creating contacts, sending confirmations, sending double confirmations, finding access to resources, and so much more. This is often an employee's full time responsibility, so volunteering to help out or pull it off yourself is *huge*. Show the organization that this is your area of expertise. Being behind the scenes provides intel on many of the key stakeholders. An example of this would be when leaders in my office wanted to host a community event so I worked with another intern and we produced the main flier for the shin-ding.

Enough about your longevity in the internship. Let's get back to the basics.

So you made it through the first four hours of your internship. You were assigned a desk and you have a phone. Well, at least yours when you are the intern sitting at that desk. You met your fellow employees and one of them was nice enough to show you where the restrooms are. Funny story, I got locked out of the office my first day because I went to run to the restroom and I was not aware there was a specific trick with the door that had to be done to keep you from getting locked out. They found me eventually.

After getting the basics down, the rubber starts to meet the road. Often it takes the technology department a few days to set up an email account and provide technology for a new intern. It took two weeks for me! I will not lie to you, this was an awkward waiting phase. Do not be socially awkward like I was. Take this time to get to know your coworkers and fill in when you can. Make it an opportunity to shine. Once you have a computer, you will be behind it and based on the type of work, many may never see anything but the top of your head behind the screen. Use this time to meet other staff members, ask others if you can assist on any projects they have, pick up some papers and assist the file clerk with filing. Whatever it takes to be seen, this is a perfect opportunity to be seen and be ambitious even if it is not the work you will be doing once access is granted. An intern needs to know everyone in the organization and what better opportunity to do so when you have the ability to bounce around. This brings up the idea of being flexible!

Some valuable traits for putting yourself out there is reminding yourself to take it one conversation at a time. For some people, being outgoing comes very easily. For others, it takes a bit more work. Set a goal for yourself. Maybe you want to have a new conversation with your coworkers 3 times a day. Maybe the following week you amp it up to four times a day. What was helpful for me was that I tried to sit at a different desk every few days so I could get to know everyone. What can an intern do to assist with being personable even when it's out of their comfort zone? Look at the internship as a no comfort zone experience in all aspects. For example, if you have strong technical publishing skills use them, but also do not put aside your lack of skills for Excel. Use the areas of strengths you have, but seek out those in the organization that are fluent in areas of weakness for you. Learning from your peers is a priceless asset. This is a time to let all guardrails down, accept that you will have to be vulnerable, and ask questions. It's important to find the right employees who can train and provide assistance on things you may need in the future. Learning Excel from a data processor in a few days will eliminate you having to take a full semester class and fit it in your schedule for a system that you may need in the future. Ask anyone who has taken an Excel class, it's worth your time to learn on the job for a grade. When you are feeling nervous, turn it into productive motivation and make the most of the available time you have. An internship will eventually end and you will no longer have access to all the experience and resources housed within that organization. I worked with multiple veterans and I wish I had taken more time to learn about the United States military from first hand perspectives.

Keep Track of What You Do!

It is critical to track all your work assignments during your internship. As some of your assignments may only pertain to this specific organization, the skills you learned from that assignment will now be a part of your own skills. All skills are valuable and will be recognizable to future employers. I made sure to keep a running note in my phone of all the things I did that day, meetings I attended, and interesting calls I received so that I could look back and reflect. Each day will turn into a week and a week will turn into a month and all of a sudden your internship is a blue. By keeping a daily journal or log of your tasks when you are doing them, you also know how to pull nice phrases from when writing about your experience on future resumes or cover letters. When it is lunch time, spend a few minutes, logging what you did in the morning, and when you get home each evening, log the activities that occurred in the afternoon.

One more critical piece to logging is also writing what you learned from that task, or who you spoke to regarding that task, or who you assisted with your assigned tasks. If you want your internship to be meaningful, you have to remember to reflect on the meaning. This record keeping will be extremely helpful if you are interning in a large corporation, but even in a small organization, it will jog your memory for future resources or networking you may need. Once the internship ends, you will not see the same people and knowing who the Excel expert is in the organization will be extremely valuable when you have to make an Excel spreadsheet in your accounting class. Additionally, journaling about the day will be a foundation for you as well as provide you the opportunity to see the skill sets you are building and enhancing for your growth and future job applications.

Mentors! Mentors! Mentors!

If you are interning in a very busy organization it may be difficult to find someone who can mentor you. This is an area that organizations sometimes forget to address. The individuals that train you on your assigned tasks, may be just the trainers and not a mentor. It is imperative that you work on finding a mentor for yourself if the organization does not provide one. A mentor is more than a trainer because they help you dig deeper and decipher what you want from your career and how to get there. An intern should not handle this task by going around to specific employees and asking them to be their mentor. This relationship should form more organically. A mentor is someone who provides insight, guidance, and assistance for your future. Once again, they may or may not be the person who trains you, but the mentor should be someone you connect with and feel comfortable with discussing future career opportunities and pathways you may be researching for your future. Having a mentor will assist the intern in working through the resources the organization can provide but also provides insight on other opportunities and skills that may help you in your future.

Do Not Forget to Set Goals for Yourself.

Early on in your internship experience, it is crucial to make some SMART goals. Smart goals are the following: Specific, measurable, achievable, relevant and time bound. Your goals may be amended or completely revised as you progress in your internship, but you do want to provide yourself with some achievable outcomes to ensure you are staying on track for your own personal and professional growth. As a requirement for your internship, you may have to make SMART goals based on what your class requirements are, but you should also have goals that you want to attain. These goals may even make you more marketable at the end of the internship as it is evident you are determined to improve and shows your quest for learning and improving your skills. It is recommended to work with your professor and your internship supervisor in writing your SMART goals to ensure you will have the appropriate opportunities to meet them. Additionally, after a few days of journaling, it is recommended to write your own SMART goals and find opportunities in the work day to meet those goals. They will make you feel accomplished and provide additional insight for your growth. An example of a SMART goal is that I wanted to increase my casework load by 50 percent by the midpoint of the summer, so each week I check in to see how I was doing with that goal.

As listening is the most important communication skill for leaders of all levels to master, a key component to a solid foundational internship is being an active listener. Sometimes you may be called into a meeting about a topic you have never encountered before. It may seem overwhelming, but if you are an active listener, you may be able to break down the key components. Use active listening skills like eye contact, body gestures, show that you are listening, avoid distractions, and give feedback or recommendations, if warranted. Being an active listener allows you to learn, to have relationships, to plan, to develop, to be part of something, to create, and to think. All these skills are essential to a successful internship.

An internship is a good opportunity to learn and make mistakes. This is an opportunity to put your coursework to work and prepare yourself for the world. The work you will do at an internship will give you time to "practice" your talents and skills and experiment with what you have learned without causing issues if you make a mistake. As we all learn from mistakes, organizations provide opportunities for the intern to be creative without causing any damage to product, concepts, or plans. Additionally, in real life we do make mistakes, and an internship is a glimpse into "a real life" profession. Use the internship as a guidebook to your strengths and areas of improvement that you may need to work on prior to applying for a full time position post graduation. If a person struggles with public speaking, this is the best opportunity to practice public speaking as much as you can. You want to utilize the staff as your own personal audience as it will improve your game and make you feel more confident.

I wanted to make one last addition to a topic that I briefly mentioned before, the gender dynamics in a work office. Being the youngest intern, and the only intern in a room full of men was not something I saw as a disadvantage, but rather an advantage. Men naturally have deeper, more booming voices, so I had great practice in utilizing my public speaking skills when needing to get the attention of the room. In addition, standing out set me apart because there was always a sense that if I did not agree on something, there was most likely a good reason and I could use it as an opportunity to practice communicating effectively. So often we land on having a "victim mentality" that because you are the only [insert any characteristic] here, that automatically means you are at a disadvantage. That could not be farther from the truth. Each room you walk into is a challenge to better yourself and better those around you.

There may be areas of the internship that are just not working for you. That is normal and acceptable, but it does not mean you cannot make it a valuable learning experience. You can take away valuable life skills when you work on something that may not be your favorite thing to do. Doing an unfavorable task will provide you with learning patience, acceptance, knowing boundaries, and how one handles stress. It is critical to take on the assigned task, push through it, think about ways that it could be improved, as this is a perfect opportunity to be innovative, and then forecast your future positions and if you want this task to be in your future. Learning comes in all shapes and sizes and even when you feel that you are not learning, you are truly learning life skills that are internal and sometimes have to be taught by experience.

Being a successful intern does not end just because you reached the maximum hours allowed for your internship. Leave on a good note! On my last day, I wrote a card to my boss to thank him for the experience and congratulate on his new position and bring in cookies. Lasting impressions are important and you never know who will work for in the future, perhaps them again!

Conclusion

In conclusion, if you take away anything important from this chapter, I want it to be these tips:

- Stay dedicated, perseverant and organized.
- Always dress for success.
- Remember your internship is an extended job interview for potential full time employment. While you are in the internship, do not be discouraged by the paycheck dilemma.
- Give 110% to your work, but do not drown in the enormity of it. Keep track of what you do!
- Find your mentor.
- Most importantly, set and achieve your goals!

V
NAILING THE INTERVIEW:
LEARNING TO PITCH YOURSELF
Madaleine Domingo

Roadmap:

Key Takeaways:
- Prepare before the interview.
- Customize your resume and cover letter to the job description, applicant profile and job listing.
- Practice a STAR or two and brainstorm a few questions you can ask the recruiter.
- Breathe, no one knows yourself better than you do! Your biggest strength is your unique, authentic personality - let's see if this internship is a right fit for both you and the recruiter.
- Visualize yourself acing the interview!
- A positive mindset will only increase your confidence which will help you succeed in real life!

"The recruiter is listening for the journey as well as the skills, attributes and characteristics that showcase your personal growth. Getting an internship is about finding the right match for both you and the recruiter."

THE TIPS FOR ACING THE INTERVIEW

Question Hook: How can you nail that internship interview?

Interviews can be nerve wracking, especially if it is your first time and you haven't had any professional training. We've put together a whole chapter designed to help you know how to get the interview, how to successfully advocate for yourself, calm your nerves, and ace the process! The more you do it, the better you'll get at it!

In an interview, you have to have empathy, curiosity and connection. *Try to put yourself in the recruiter's shoes:* What would be the ideal candidate in their eyes? What kinds of qualities are needed to succeed in this role based on the job description? Once you figure out those things, think about the ways in which you are a good fit, and tell that to the interviewer. Interviews are interpersonal, and they require a risk of meeting a stranger, and trust in letting the stranger into their space. Be cognizant of the energy you give off when you approach the meeting place! As a general rule of thumb, even a simple smile can brighten someone's day and you never know who you might be smiling at :)

The Elevator Pitch

Picture this: You are at a networking function at your university and you are meeting people who are in your desired career field. How do you introduce yourself in the short span of time you have to speak with them? An elevator pitch is your personal pitch in a networking opportunity that should last the amount of time you might spend in an elevator! It is a quick 30-45 second summary introduction to you, your interests, and a great way to highlight your unique qualities.

Elevator pitches are useful at professional mixers and

asking for informational interviews (people might need some information about you before they agree to doing one). Most importantly, elevator pitches can be used as an answer for the classic, vague job interview question: "tell me about yourself".

Follow this elevator pitch script outline and then look at an example to help you think about your own elevator pitch!

Script Outline

Hi! I am "give your full name"
1. Degree/Areas of study
2. Experience (accomplishments vs. jobs; *jobs might not reflect who you are)
3. Top qualities you bring to the table
4. Opportunities in which you are interested
5. Give your business card (YES, make some!) and tell them you are interested in making contacts. For example: "Here's my card! I am always looking to expand my network so if you know of anyone who I should speak to about my goals or possible opportunities, I'd really appreciate it." (hand them your business card)

*Tip: Shake the person's hand at the start of your interaction, smile, and maintain eye contact.

Example: Here's an example of what I might say in an elevator pitch...

1. *"Hi! My name is Maddy Domingo (shake the person's hand).*
2. *I am an undergraduate student at the University of San Diego double majoring in Political Science and Communication Studies.*
3. *My recent year studying abroad coupled with my extensive research in both my fields of study has led me to develop the beginnings of a global perspective that I hope to build upon in my aspirations in foreign*

service.

4. *I am currently interning with the State Department in the Virtual Student Federal Service (VSFS) Program where I create and execute English language learning lesson plans for high school learners. My experience with VSFS has instilled in me a passion for education and intercultural communication, and has helped me develop leadership and both oral and written communication skills.*

5. *Here's my card, I'm always looking to expand my network to find new opportunities. If you think of anything or know of someone I could speak to, I'd really appreciate it! (hand them your business card)."*

The Recruitment Process

Here's what to expect when you go through the internship application process:

1. Soliciting: When the company puts out an ad/job listing about the job to attract applicants
2. Screening: Eliminate some candidates who are obviously not a good fit
3. Determining: Selecting the person
4. Offering: When the company gives you an offer!

The STAR Method

Your life is a story that ebbs and flows. The trick is to be able to think about the moments you want to share and be able to share them in an engaging way. Check out the STAR method to help you frame your life stories in an interview. This strategy is good for interview questions like "tell me about a time when..."

Follow this STAR method script outline and then look at an example to help you think about your own STAR's!

Script Outline

1. Situation: Give a brief overview of the circumstances
2. Task: What were you faced with/challenged by?
3. Action: What did you do in response to your situation? For example, "I created a google sheet for all interns to log their time slots so there was no scheduling confusion or overlap"
4. Result: "As a result..." share the outcome, for example "As a result, I learned the importance of working in a team, which I intend to continue at _____ company/organization"

It is *vital* after you finish explaining your story to remember to tie it back to how your story/the lessons you learned are relevant to the job. The recruiter is listening for the journey and also the skills, attributes and characteristics that showcase your personal growth. Characteristics like dependability, a team player, positivity and intrinsic motivation are just a few attractive qualities to keep in mind.

Example: Here's an example of a STAR you might give in an interview...

"When I worked at Mary's Pizza Shack as a cashier over the summer, a frustrated customer walked into the shop. The customer started yelling because their pizza had sausage on it instead of pepperoni. The customer started banging his fist on the counter, disrupting the ambiance of the restaurant. I started by personally apologizing to the customer that their pizza was made incorrectly and I asked the chef to make them a new one. My colleague and I stood together and politely asked the customer to take a seat while the pizza was cooking, and the customer obliged.

It was through this experience that I learned the importance of working in a team and the importance of clear communication skills when things don't go as planned. I intend to utilize these skills as an intern at your company in order to create a positive, collaborative work environment."

Research and Preparation: Job Listing, Job Description, and Applicant Profile

Once you know what internship you want to pursue, it's time to prepare! There are a few documents that you will most likely come across...here's what you need to know.

The Job Listing serves to attract candidates to apply for the position, and is most likely used to post on the company's website or social media to advertise the position's availability. The listing will include highlights of what the job entails and the skills or characteristics that are associated with the job. This document is meant to sell the position or organization, so keep a keen eye on the information to see if you would be a good fit.

The Applicant Profile describes the ideal candidate for a position, clearly listing the desired skills/traits needed for the job. In some cases a computer might execute the preliminary screening of applicants to cut people who are clearly not qualified. The computer will scan your resume and cover letter looking for buzz words including competencies, behaviors, talents, abilities and work experience that were advertised in the applicant profile. Or you might be invited to answer questions in an automated online video interview, which is programmed to look for these buzzwords in your responses. The manager of the hiring process normally creates the applicant profile, so pay attention to what they are looking for!

The Job Description goes into a lot more detail about the internship itself, the roles and responsibilities expected, benefits, perks, compensation, and requirements. This document is updated regularly and is used as the foundation for creating the job listing.

Why are these pieces of documentation important? Success in landing that internship is based on research. Don't take resume, cover letter and interview prep lightly, because the more you understand the position, the better you can sell yourself as the ideal candidate while showcasing your life experiences that are attractive to the recruiter. Preparation is key.

The Candidate Package: Resume, Cover Letter, Reference Page

Once you know you are going to go for it, you will most likely be asked to submit a few documents including a resume, cover letter, and/or reference page. The trick is to customize your documents to the job listing, applicant profile, and job description. Make sure it is easy to scan your information. The recruiter may only spend a few seconds with it on the first round of recruiting. The goal of the candidate package is to land that interview!

Resume: A one-page document that includes
- Your name, phone number, and e-mail address
- A brief career objective: A sentence describing what you want to *give* the recruiter, for example:
  - "I am looking for a cultural affairs management position where I can apply my training in political science and communications studies, coupled with my experience studying abroad, to provide a global perspective"
  - OR "I am looking for a management position in cultural affairs to create and implement staff development and cultural identity training activities that are inspired by my experience studying abroad"
- Your education, involvements, scholarships, work experience, volunteer experience

Debunking common resume myths:

MYTH: Recruiters are only interested in paid experience
No! Recruiters are looking for the skills/attributes/lessons that have come out of your life experiences. Volunteer experience especially related to your career field can showcase passion and dedication to your work.

<u>MYTH: One resume can be submitted to all job listings</u>
Not the case! You must tailor your resume to the requirements of the specific job listing. For example, if the job description is requiring experience in education, make sure to include any tutoring experience or possible experience teaching English. Taking that extra step will show the recruiter that you are a good fit for the position and also showcase your interest and care for your application.

<u>MYTH: Your resume should include all of your work experience</u>
Correction! Resumes should include all of your *relevant* work experience. It is okay to leave out a position that isn't relevant to the job you are applying to.

<u>MYTH: A resume should only be black and white</u>
Think again! Where are you applying to? If it is for a creative position, show them your creativity in the formatting of your resume! As long as all of the necessary information is there, show them the creative pizzazz they're looking for!

Cover Letter: This document is your chance to talk to the recruiter, and for them to get a sense of your professionality, tone, and experience. Keep it short and sweet, 3-4 paragraphs max. Here's a few things to keep in mind:

1. *Why are you contacting them?*
   "I'm writing to you about the _____ position I found on LinkedIn"
2. *Hype yourself up!* You are a unique person. Tell them why they should be interested in getting to know you more!
   "I believe you will be especially interested in my experience in _____"
   "After reading about your company's challenge in _____, I believe you will want to hear about my experience in _____"

3. *Briefly explain why you are suited for the job*, just enough to get them interested! Remember, your goal in these documents is to get that interview!
4. *Showcase your interest.* Wrap it up by sharing with them your interest in the position, and ask for an interview to get to know each other.

Your cover letter, resume, and references should have the same letterhead so that it will be easy for recruiters to identify your documents during the hectic hiring process! Make it easier on them so that your application won't get overlooked.

Reference Page: If asked, this is a short document that includes the names of at least three people who can be contacted if the recruiter has any questions about you. Remember to let your recommenders know prior to submitting your reference page that they are being listed! Simply include their name, contact information (email or phone number), their relationship to you, and a quick point about what they can speak about in regards to your character or work experience. For example:

Olga Strizhkina
VSFS Education USA Russia Mentor
Virtual Student Federal Service

Ms. Strizhkina is my mentor as an intern for the U.S. State Department at the Education USA Russia program who can speak to my experience in an international education setting, my organizational skills, as well as my ability to prioritize, manage and complete multiple tasks effectively with a high level of efficiency.

Office: (000) 000-000
Email: xxx

General Advice

- Sometimes writing positively about yourself can be awkward. To combat these common sentiments, pretend like you are writing to a good friend who knows your character. Don't worry! Advocating for yourself is necessary in the hiring process.
- Consider using an online service to compare your resume to the job listing, as this could improve your chances to make it past an automated or human screener. JobScan offers a free scan at www.jobscan.co
- Brainstorm: Before you crush that interview, make sure you set aside some time to brainstorm likely questions you might be asked. What kind of skills/qualities/characteristics/requirements do they require as seen in the job listing and job description? Also, think about how you, as a recruiter, might probe those answers out of candidates. What kinds of questions will help the recruiter find the best fit candidate?
- STAR's: Think about what kinds of stories might be relevant to share within the context of the job description! Ponder those STAR's, maybe write them down, or practice them in front of a mirror!
- Questions: Make sure you have a few questions in your back pocket to ask the recruiter! Think of a few before you head in there. Recruiters love to see your investment in the company through previous research you bring to the interview, along with interesting questions.

What to Do About Nerves

If you feel those anxious butterflies start to act up, try practicing one of these relaxation techniques:

- *Cognitive restructuring / Stretching*: Doing some stretching the day of your interview can help blood flow. If you have time after you arrive at the building of your interview, take a second to stretch out your muscles. Try moving your neck around slowly, bend over to try to touch your toes and let your body relax in a big stretch. Massage your cheeks and stretch your jaw for annunciation.

- *Visualization:* Try to visualize your interview going well before you go in. The more positively oriented you are about the outcome of the interview, the more likely your confidence will boost, and bye-bye butterflies!

- *Breathing:* Most importantly, don't forget to *breathe*! Take three deep breaths to center yourself in the moment, and believe you are ready to go! Remember that no one knows you better than you do, so go in there and showcase your unique person! When you try and make yourself fit in the candidate mold you think the hiring manager is looking for, you risk hiding your biggest asset - yourself! Let's say you fake who you are in an interview, and you get hired. Now you're stuck in a job when your boss thinks you are someone you are not. Getting an internship is about finding the right match for both you and the hiring manager. *Go for it! You miss 100% of the shots you don't take!!* You are unique, and you have unique attributes to offer, so be your authentic self!

- *Practice:* If you want to practice what it might be like in an interview, check out any of the online resources to practice. Using online systems like InterviewBuddy allows you to practice interviewing in a realistic setting. InterviewBuddy is a user-friendly online mock interview system that allows you to join a virtual mock interview wherever you are. Ask your school if they can give you free access to this tool! If not, $18 is worth giving it a shot! With InterviewBuddy, you receive a scorecard highlighting your strengths and weaknesses after your 25-minute interview, and access to the recording for your own reflections. If not, I highly recommend asking a friend to sit down with you and ask you some standard questions you might find in an interview. You could even record yourself with your computer or on Zoom to see how you look and respond to questions. Read on to check out some examples of these!

- o https://interviewbuddy.in/

Why Study Abroad?

Study abroad is one of the most popular opportunities for college students around the world. USD prides itself on their study abroad involvement and participation, and markets study abroad to prospective students and families. Studying abroad is one of the best opportunities to get to know yourself through experiences like culture shock, intercultural communication, and global awareness and perspective.

My Study Abroad Experience

I studied abroad during my junior year, one semester in Madrid, Spain, and another on Semester at Sea. I was constantly in unfamiliar circumstances, dealing with language barriers and intercultural communication that only encouraged me to practice my communication skills and further develop networking skills. You never know who you are going to meet when you put yourself outside of your comfort zone. That can change your life! Not to mention networking opportunities...if you ask around, you might find someone who knows someone who is currently working in your desired career field.

Two of my letters of recommendation for a post-grad opportunity were from people I met or was connected to while I was abroad! Don't be afraid to shake hands with a stranger and give them a quick elevator pitch if you see an opportunity. I strongly believe that people are inherently kind; they will want to give of themselves to help you out!

My Internship and Even MORE Tips!

I am currently interning for the U.S. Department of State: Virtual Student Federal Service, EducationUSA Russia. My mentor is from Russia, and although she speaks fluent English, I came across a few instances in which I had to better communicate my thoughts for her to understand. My interview went well because I reacted to the language barrier by immediately slowing down my speech, annunciating more, and completely explaining my thought processes, leaving little room for confusion. I did all of those without getting uncomfortable or nervous. Why? Because it was an amazing opportunity to be interviewed for such a beautiful intercultural position! I channeled my excitement and gratitude and had some fun. I attribute my acceptance into the program to my energy and adaptability during the interview which is vital to be a successful English teacher and mentor as mentioned in the job description.

You're in luck! Even more tips. Yes, you're welcome!

- *Start early.* Apply for internships and jobs while you are still in college. The more you practice the entire process, from getting dressed properly to answering questions about yourself, the better you will get at it. Don't get frustrated if your first internship opportunity falls through...use your experience to do better at the next one!
- *Dress appropriately!* Check out the vibes of the company you are interviewing with to curtail your attire to their company culture. However, it is safe to assume that business casual is the best way to make a good first impression. You are being watched the second you pull into the parking lot, and you never know who you might bump into that might have a sway in the hiring process, so be on your best behavior!
- *Get to know yourself!* Try out a Myers Briggs personality test, and see what your strengths and weaknesses are according to the test (which may or may not be 100% accurate). In the interview, showcase your strengths and don't be afraid to talk about your weaknesses and how you have handled them in the past. Everyone makes mistakes. What is most

important is how you can talk about those mistakes and showcase growth and commitment.

- *Take advantage of the opportunities around you!* On campus career fairs are a great way to practice networking and become familiar with the rhythm of a recruiter conversation.
- *Speak slowly and enunciate.* Give a few tongue twisters a go before you walk into the interview!

ASK QUESTIONS! Be a good active listener! One of the biggest ways to stand out against the other interviewees is to ask questions that showcase your curiosity and interest in the position. Show the recruiter you have thought about what has been said, and you are curious to learn more.

- Good questions might consist of
  - What is the biggest challenge the company has faced in the last three years, and how did you combat it?
  - What would you say is the best part about working for the company?
  - How would you describe the employee culture at the company?
  - Clarification Questions: Ask that burning question you need in order to make something clearer! You only have a certain amount of allotted time, so take advantage of it!

Conclusion

Congrats! You made it to the end of the chapter! Remember you always have this to come back to as an outline for when you are going through the internship process. We have discussed the candidate package including a resume, cover letter, reference page, job listing, job description, applicant profile, what to do about nerves, the STAR method, the elevator pitch, study abroad and overviewed general tips and information. When you've done the preparation, there's only one thing left to do: smile and walk in with your head held high! Shake off those nerves and be proud of yourself! Remember you are in an exciting moment of opportunity!

Further Reading

- *Getting to Yes* by William Ury & Roger Fisher
- *How to Answer Interview Questions* by Peggy McKee
- *What to Say in Every Job Interview* by Carole Martin

VI
HOW TO NETWORK: EXPANDING YOUR PROFESSIONAL HORIZON
Saleena Ordorica

Roadmap:
    i.   Making the Connection
    ii.   Discovering Your Network
    iii.   Personalizing Your Internship
    iv.   Leveraging Your Virtual Network
    v.   Preparing for a Successful Networking Experience
    vi.   Maintaining Your Network
    vii.   Conclusion

Key Takeaways:

- *Networking can help you find an internship:* Networking is one of the most important skills to practice in acquiring an internship and will allow you to expand your social network and connect with individuals within your career field.
- *Networking can happen almost anywhere:* You can always turn any interaction into an opportunity to form a professional connection with someone when appropriate.
- *Networking is circular:* After learning how to form professional connections with individuals who can help you, you will eventually become a resource for others to learn and benefit from.

"Networking involves being intentional about who you want to make connections with and staying informed about what is happening in your career field."

Networking is a skill that is important to continue developing and utilizing throughout the entirety of your professional journey. Networking involves being intentional about who you want to make connections with and staying informed about what is happening in your career field. The network you create for yourself will only continue to grow and become more valuable as you gain more professional experience. Maintaining this important skill will not only help you continue advancing your skill set, but will also allow you to expand the opportunities available to you.

Making the Connection

One of the most fundamental parts of the process in searching for an internship is networking. Networking is the process of forming connections and professional relationships with individuals and organizations that can help you advance your career. Networking is a skill that is not only important to practice in the beginning stages of acquiring an internship, but is also something that should be maintained even after the completion of the internship. Similar to making new friends or acquaintances, social connections can be made almost anywhere. While networking might appear to be a daunting task for some people, it is truly one of the best ways to gain personal insight into your career field. Additionally, this process does not always have to take place in a formal setting. These types of social connections can be formed in all types of environments as long as one is willing and able to step out of their comfort zone and initiate the interaction. This chapter will serve as a helpful guide in laying out the various steps involved in the process of networking and interacting with others to expand your professional horizon.

Some of the most beneficial connections you can make typically involve the individuals that you find yourself surrounded by the most. Beginning with individuals you know can be a great first step in learning how to navigate the process of networking by practicing and getting more comfortable with these types of interactions. When thinking about the type of people you want to network with, it is important to start with those who are most accessible to you and then slowly work your way up by branching out to others. Most times, the individuals you know will be able to help you make further connections by introducing you to other people they know who can be a great resource for you as well. This is the best and simplest way to begin building your social network. When trying to figure out what types of connections you should be making, it is important to aim to interact with those who share your similar interests and have the type of professional experiences you may be interested in pursuing in the future.

Discovering Your Network

Expanding your professional network involves stepping back and taking the time to think about the social environments you spend most of your time in. For example, students in high school or college might begin by speaking to their professors, advisors, and even their peers in the classroom to help learn more about the opportunities that are available to them. While social networking may occur in a group setting at times, taking the time to set up one-on-one interactions with individuals you think can provide you with career advice and support can be very helpful. With these types of meetings, you can take the time to dive deeper into sharing about each others' experiences as well as asking the questions you are most interested in learning more about. Having these conversations can help you build on your career goals and continue shaping the way you will engage with future professionals.

Know who you are talking to!

One thing to keep in mind before initiating these interactions is to make sure you come prepared with specific questions and topics you would like to discuss and learn more about. With this, it is important to take into consideration who the individual is that you will be speaking with. Depending on how well you know about their professional background and experience, it could be useful to do some additional research to figure out what specific areas they could be of most assistance with. This can be done by doing a simple search on the internet with the intent of finding their professional biographies. In addition to discussing your goals and career interests, these interactions can even be a good opportunity to ask about what a career in the field you are interested in looks like. If the person you are speaking with does not have the specific experience you are looking for, chances are that they have someone within their own professional network that they can connect you with. The most important thing to remember during these conversations is to not be afraid to ask questions, even if you are asking them to help connect you with someone else they know. Additionally, the individuals you choose to connect with are always willing to help you reach your goals because they too were once in your position trying to navigate the internship search. The process of networking comes full circle because once you learn how to form these connections, you will eventually become a resource for others to utilize as well down the road.

Networking can also be a great way to assess where you stand in the job pool by assessing your skills and qualifications. When you speak with others who are in your career field, you start to get a better idea of what types of skills and experiences might be beneficial to have in order to present yourself as a competitive candidate for the position you are most interested in. This can be very helpful in terms of figuring out what type of internship will be the best fit for you. In fact, this is a great step towards not only building your experience on your resume, but also developing the skills necessary to be a better fit for the job you want in the future. With this, it is important to take the time to research different internship positions carefully and determine not only which one fits your interests the best, but also the one that will be able to offer you the most valuable experience to continue advancing your skill set. Additionally, it can be helpful to look into the type of individuals who work for the organization or company you are interested in. This will give you an idea of the pool of potential individuals who you can eventually interact with and who can become part of your own professional network. After determining which places you are most interested in interning at, it could also be helpful to reach out to current employees. Most times, organizations will have a group of specific individuals who remain specifically in charge of the internship program. If this is the case, it can be helpful to reach out to these particular individuals beforehand to connect with them and see what that relationship might look like if you are offered an internship.

Personalizing Your Internship Experience

Once you have accepted an internship position with an organization or company you are happy with, the next step is to look for someone who might be willing to serve as your personal mentor. This might be intimidating to do when you first come into a new position where everyone knows one another and already has an established routine. Therefore, setting small networking goals can assist you in making a few connections with other employees and then expanding from there. Once you have gotten to know a couple of people, this might give you an idea of who you would like to learn more from. If the internship does not already involve providing you with a specific mentor, asking an individual to mentor you not only demonstrates your willingness to expand your knowledge, but also helps personalize your internship experience. Personalizing your internship is important as it ensures that you are getting exactly what you need out of this experience. Before finding a mentor, it is also important to figure out what exactly you are looking to get out of this relationship and ensuring that the person you select is capable of helping you. This involves complete transparency when connecting with potential mentors in terms of asking not only whether they are able to help you achieve your goals, but also if they have the time and effort to truly dedicate themselves to you as a mentor.

Once you begin your internship, you can further expand your network by asking to work in different areas within the organization or company. If someone asks for help completing additional tasks or with a bigger project, it would be of interest to volunteer and ask if you can be assigned to these areas. The more places you are able to work in, the more opportunities you will have to meet new people and facilitate these professional connections. Additionally, if the place you are interning for has more interns, it would also be beneficial to network with these individuals as well. Whether or not these individuals can provide you what you are looking for is not as important. Rather, broadening your network with individuals who match your experience level can be effective in terms of learning about their other work experiences that could provide you with useful insight. Lastly, most individuals will likely be in similar situations in terms of being new to the job search and this can help reduce further stress and anxiety through being able to share and confide in each other about your current experiences and challenges.

Leveraging Your Virtual Network

So far, we have discussed the more traditional approach to networking for an internship. However, as we move forward, we will also explore additional ways in which one can expand their network virtually. The next form of networking can involve using social media and different internet forums to connect with others about job opportunities. Job websites, such as LinkedIn, provide one with the opportunity to promote themselves online through the creation of a professional profile in order to market themselves to a greater audience. Networking online through websites like this can allow you to network with a much more diverse group of people than you might find simply in your own social environments. Additionally, networking is much easier to do online as you can easily create connections with individuals by sending them friend requests and personalized messages that can help you reach individuals from all parts of the world. Using these online resources can help introduce you to individuals that can be vital connections to job opportunities you are interested in and keep you more informed about the types of organizations and companies that exist within your particular career field. Whether or not you are looking to make direct connections with individuals, apps such as LinkedIn provide you with important information about individuals that can help you learn more about them in order to help you also prepare for potential in-person interactions with them. Overall, networking is possible almost anywhere and utilizing online resources that are available can help you significantly expand your professional network and meet individuals who can connect you with the opportunities you are most interested in.

When it comes to thinking about how one might effectively form connections with others, it is important to take into consideration a couple of things. First, before attempting to create any types of professional connections, either online or in-person, you should do some research on the company or organization to find out which specific areas your skills and interests align the most with. Networking involves being intentional about who you want to make connections with and staying informed about what is happening in your career field. With this, it is important to try and find employees who share similarities with you. This can include going to the same school, having the same interests, or even having similar connections with others. The objective here is to find areas that you have in common with others to help better facilitate a more personal and thoughtful interaction. In doing so, you are increasing your chances of getting this person's attention and receiving a response from them. If you decide to network with others in this specific manner, some information you might include in your message to them might be: your name and school, your shared interests/connections with them (i.e. individuals that you both know), and what interests you about them in terms of how they might be able to help you advance your career.

One important thing to note is that not all connections you form will introduce you directly to professional career opportunities. Rather, networking is a process that takes time and each interaction will lead you to new insight you did not know before. Sometimes the people we are directly connected with through our social environments will be able to help us with certain job opportunities. However, this is not always the case. This is where it becomes important to practice engaging in these professional interactions with others because sometimes you might have to search for someone who has the experience you need to connect you with the opportunity you are looking for. By continuing to practice this very important skill, you will eventually come to develop a certain style of networking that works for you so that you can continue to build confidence in yourself and your ability to make connections with other professionals. Another way to discover potential connections is to find events, either in-person or virtual, to attend that can help introduce you to individuals with your similar interests. These events can be anything ranging from career fairs to more simple events, such as lectures or discussions, about a topic that interests you. Whether or not you find someone who can help connect you directly to a professional opportunity is not as important as forming connections with other people who can provide you with some of their own personal insight and experiences to help you in your career journey.

Preparing for a Successful Networking Experience

We have discussed the importance of going outside of your comfort zone to continue to network with others. However, this next part involves tips on how to network in a way that is most effective for you. Attending more formal networking events, such as career fairs and hiring events, can be hectic at first since there will most likely be a lot of people in attendance. With this, it is important to prepare ahead of time since you will most likely only get a short period of time to network with the individuals or organization/company you are most interested in. Before attending a network event, you should do some research on the organizations and companies you are interested in and come prepared with specific questions you have about the job. This can help facilitate a smoother conversation between you and the recruitment team and show them what you are particularly interested in. It can also be helpful for any type of networking, especially at events like career fairs and hiring events, to practice a short "elevator pitch" that you can use to properly and efficiently introduce yourself to potential employers and relay to them the qualities about yourself that you want them to know. Within this short introduction, you can tell them about your educational background and previous work experiences and professional skill set. Also, coming into the conversation with an idea of what position or department you are most interested in demonstrates to the recruiter that you have done your research and know exactly what interests you in their company or organization. In addition to preparing for your conversations with potential employers, it can be useful to come with a resume and a business card, if you have it, so that you can easily provide them with your contact information and professional experience for future reference. Coming prepared with these items shows the employer that you are very interested in the opportunities they have to offer and demonstrates your willingness and motivation to pursue a career with them in the near future. You should remember to dress accordingly for these types of events and come in business attire to project an image of professionalism to your potential future employers. Overall, the most important thing to remember is to not only be professional in your interactions, but also to be comfortable in showcasing who you are as a person and as a strong candidate for the position.

For students actively looking for ways to expand their social network, exploring on-campus organizations can help individuals discover new communities where they can branch out further and learn more about their particular career field or industry. Some organizations that have become more popular within the college environment are professional fraternities. These organizations typically are focused around a particular field of study or profession, such as medicine, business, engineering, etc. that provide them with specific guidance and opportunities to advance themselves in this particular career. Joining these types of organizations can help you get better connected with your student peers and other like-minded individuals and expand your leadership and networking skills. By joining an organization with people who share your same career interests, you can learn about how other individuals plan to utilize their degree and discover new ways to enhance your own professional development. Typically, a major perk of joining these professional fraternities involves getting access to exclusive networking opportunities within your particular field. Taking advantage of these career-specific communities around you can greatly assist you in your journey towards obtaining the career of your dreams.

Maintaining Your Network

In any opportunity you have to network with other professionals it is important to exchange contact information to help maintain the connection made. By doing so, you will be able to stay in touch with those you have made connections with and can potentially reach out again if you find that they can be a helpful resource for you throughout your professional journey. One way to help facilitate this is to follow up after the networking event and send them a message expressing your gratitude for taking the time to connect with you as well as your hope to remain in touch and advise you of any opportunities they might know of that could benefit you. Maintaining communication is even more important following the completion of an internship. Those who you have direct experience working with can serve as great references in the future for potential employment opportunities. These are the individuals that can speak directly to your particular work ethic and skill set. By maintaining a positive relationship with employees from your internship, you keep the door open for future communication that can. Among the ways you can keep in touch include sending a follow-up message or email to your internship supervisor, connecting with them online through LinkedIn, and even inviting them out in a more social context to continue strengthening the relationship and exchanging any additional ideas or feedback you might have regarding your position in the internship.

The biggest aspect to networking following an internship is to keep track of the people you have formed connections with. One way to help with this involves keeping a list of the contacts you have made and taking note of who the person is and their position, what types of experiences they have had, and anything else that stood out during your encounter with them. This will help serve as a refresher any time you wish to look back at your list and determine which individuals might be best suited to help you. Your path towards finding a career can be complex and challenging at times. Therefore, it is important to keep yourself organized when it comes to networking so that you can make the most out of your professional network. Every single person you connect with will offer some sort of value to your own personal insight and knowledge about your career. The connections your form with individuals are made more meaningful when you actually put in the effort to continue maintaining them over time. This can help you gain greater recognition by your employer and will help them remember you better if you choose to apply for a job at the company or use them as a reference in the future.

Networking can also help diversify your own perspective and provide you with insights you may not have known or thought of before. Sometimes you will meet people who have very different ideas and interests than you. However, just because they may not be able to help you achieve your specific career goals does not mean the relationship is not beneficial to you. These individuals whose ideas diverge from your own are just as important as the connections you make with those who share your similar interests. In fact, these individuals can help you continue to develop your skills and knowledge and explore different areas in the workplace. You may even find these individuals can help support you in other ways that involve understanding the challenges that come with searching for a job in general.

Conclusion

Networking is a skill that will take time to practice and develop over time. This is a skill you will be able to utilize throughout your entire career journey that will help you get to where you want to be in life. More importantly, it is imperative to engage in networking before, during, and after the completion of your internship. All stages are crucial to building different connections that will be able to guide you in the right direction in your career path. Networking is a skill that eventually comes full circle and you will eventually grow and find yourself to be someone else's future important connection who is just starting out as you once were. The practice of making connections and networking only continues to develop over time, even when you finally find a job that you are passionate about. Life will always involve meeting new people and connections will never cease at any point in time. Your professional network will continue to expand and follow you throughout your entire life. It is important to be open to connecting with others no matter what and be open to the idea of putting yourself out there, even if the outcome is not what you hoped for. Networking will reveal a variety of opportunities for you that you may have never experienced before or even knew existed. It is important to continue working on this skill so that you can continue making meaningful relationships with others and diversify your skill set to continue improving as a professional.

PART THREE

Vital Perspectives

VII
TRANSCENDING BORDERS: THE TIPS I WISH I KNEW AS AN INTERNATIONAL STUDENT
Namie Yazaki

Roadmap:

Key Takeaways:
- This chapter is for international students who want to obtain an internship or get a job in the U.S..
- Every international student who wants either an internship or a job will have to go through some type of process, which is typically very complicated and overwhelming.
- I will discuss how I got an internship as an international student, some work visas that international students are required to obtain, and share some of my tips for international students based on my experience as an international student.

"Looking for a job, collecting information, and making connections at the same time are not easy, and it can be overwhelming."

Introduction

Getting an internship or job is already difficult and time-consuming, but doing this as an international student is even more difficult and takes even more time. This is because international students need to worry about obtaining a work visa, and additional restrictions here in the United States (U.S.). This is also the case for those who want to work in the U.S. after graduation. It is important to note that in order to receive these visas, companies need to sponsor individuals, and not every company can sponsor a work visa, so this is an additional disadvantage for international students. Getting a visa is not automatic after you get a job. One needs to submit documents, and then win a lottery. I did not know this information until recently.

My name is Namie, an international student from Japan. I am studying at the University of San Diego, studying for a Master of Arts in International Relations. I came to the United States almost two years ago, and I did not know about any visa system until I started looking for job opportunities. However, once I started learning more about the U.S. visa system, I wondered why I did not know about this system beforehand. But after learning more, I understood that there are too many restrictions for international students, which means that there are less opportunities compared to American students, since not every company can take care of work visas.

As an international student, I have struggled with these things and I am still struggling. I had to collect this information all by myself. I learned that there is not much advice or discussion on how international students can access internships in the U.S. and because of this it was hard to go through this process alone, but it was an essential part of my career path. Looking for a job, collecting the needed information, and making important connections at the same time is not easy, and it can be overwhelming. I also recognize that it is okay to fear and stress how daunting all those tasks are. But you are not alone! In this chapter, I will give tips for how to navigate the system for international students who will face the same challenges, so that they do not feel overwhelmed like myself. It is my intention to provide information that will help international students have a better understanding of the visa and job hunting processes!

Getting an Internship as an International Student

How Did I Get My Internship?

I am currently an intern for a Non Profit Organization (NPO), called ASCENDtials. This is a San Diego based organization, focusing on providing educational knowledge for BIPOC (Black, Indigenous, and People of Color) communities. I found this organization on VolunteerMatch, since I was looking for a volunteer role which was related to media and politics. I was interested and amazed by how the media can affect people's political thoughts, so I looked for a role and field that would work in both media and politics. I did not plan to stay long when I started volunteering with ASCENDtials, but once I started working and getting involved with the tasks that I was performing, I greatly enjoyed it and decided I wanted to stay. My original plan was just to volunteer during the summer break, but then, the founder of the organization offered me to work as an intern, so I accepted and continued with the organization. While I did not expect to obtain an internship with the same organization I volunteered for, I would recommend this as a good strategy for those interested in securing an internship. This is a good strategy because this demonstrates commitment and loyalty to an organization that can lead to meaningful connections and opportunity.

Getting a Crucial Practical Training (CPT) Visa for an Internship

For international students, a CPT visa is required in order to obtain an internship. If you do not have one, you are not authorized to work in the U.S.. The application process is simple, you just need to visit a website from your university's international office to apply. As long as you are accepted by a company/institution and have an internship offer letter, you have all that you need. It does not take much time to get approved, it usually takes less than a week. Unfortunately, there are also restrictions for international students who do find an internship. For example, international students are only allowed to work within the semester, and only can work a maximum of 20 hours per week. Therefore, in my case, I worked for four hours every day from Monday through Friday.

If you have questions or concerns about this visa process, I highly recommend visiting the international office at your university, and speaking with the advisors. The advisors at this type of office are experts in these visas, so you can ask them any and all questions and concerns about your visas. The international offices also provide international students with information about events regarding work visas, and I highly recommend international students attend events like these. I joined one of the online workshops from my university's international office, and this event made me realize that it is not easy for international students to secure a job in the U.S.. I also found this event to be very motivational because I learned that I was not the only student who was facing these struggles.

Information on Visas for International Students

Optional Practical Training (OPT) Visa

OPT visas are available to international students after they graduate with a master's degree. With this visa, you can have multiple jobs at the same time. Students can start applying for an OPT visa as early as their last semester of their program. However, it can take three months, and sometimes even up to six months to get an OPT visa, so I recommend you to apply for it as soon as you can.

For students studying science, technology, engineering or mathematics (STEM), the OPT visa is valid for up to three years; however, for students studying humanities, they can only have an OPT visa for up to one year. Hence, the OPT visa is a little disadvantageous for those who are studying humanities. One can work with an OPT visa, however, not every company hires employees with these visas. Think about it this way, if someone says they can only work for one year, how likely is a company to hire the person? Most companies might say no, since hiring someone new already costs a lot and they want the person to stay as long as possible. Therefore, looking for a company that hires people with OPT visas can be difficult and time consuming, but at the same time one of the best options for international students.

Work Visas:H1B/H1B Cap Exemption

Getting a job which accepts an OPT visa is already hard; however, it is even more difficult if you want to keep working in the U.S. after your OPT visa expires. This means you need to find a company or institution which accepts OPT visas, plus is willing to sponsor a work visa for you. This can be overwhelming! Thus, if you are an international student who is interested in working in the U.S. after you graduate, I highly recommend you get an internship with a company or institution that can sponsor your visa. This is because the work visas, H1B and H1B cap exemption, are very competitive, and it can take a lot of time and effort to get a job from a company or institution that is willing to sponsor your visa. Moreover, if you can get an internship with a company or institution that then becomes a full time job, this will allow you to not worry about looking for a job at another company, and can save you time and trouble. Getting a job with an OPT visa, and looking for a job which will provide you H1B/H1B Cap Exemption can be another option, but if you do not want to worry and being stressed about your work status, get an internship first! Especially for those students studying humanities, it is important to remember that one does not have many chances to apply for the H1B lottery in comparison to those students majoring in STEM.

Getting employment from a company or institution that will sponsor your work visa does not mean you will get the visa. It is tricky, but there is a reason why this happens. This is because there are too many applications for H1B visas almost every year, so you need to win a lottery. This lottery is only once a year. According to the United States' Office of Citizenship and Immigration Services, there were about 480,000 applications last year, but only 65,000 of them were selected (very competitive!). Some people can get a H1B visa just by applying for the lottery only once, but there are also some people who might have to apply for the H1B lottery several times to win. For those who apply for the lottery several times, it can take them several years to get the work visa. You can apply for the lottery as many times, but you might have to go back to your home country until you are authorized to work in the U.S..

International students who are obtaining their master's degree have better chances, but it is still competitive. 20,000 H1B visas are guaranteed for students with master's degrees (Prodigy Finance). Also, students with master's degrees have two chances to try the lottery, however, it is still very competitive. The deadline for the submission to this specific visa is in mid-March, and there are several documents that one needs to apply for the lottery. This means if you want to work for a company which will help you get an H1B visa, you need to be accepted by the company before March meaning that it is imperative to start job hunting as early as possible, since that process alone can take a lot of time. Lastly, it is also important to note that the information required for these work visas might change every year, therefore, be sure to visit the international office at your university regularly to be updated on the information.

What is H1B Cap Exemption?

There are two types of H1B visas: the H1B and the H1B Cap Exemption. The H1B cap exemption is a little different from H1B in that this visa is for someone who works for higher educational institutions or NPOs. There is no lottery system for H1B Cap Exemption unlike the usual H1B, and there is no annual deadline to apply for it. H1B Cap Exemptions might sound easier to apply, however, this visa is designed for higher educational institutions and NPOs, meaning it is still difficult to get an opportunity as it relies on the institutions.

Online Platforms and Tools That Are Friendly for International Students

Here are some useful online platforms that can support you with your job hunting experience. These platforms below are the ones that were recommended to me by staff members from my university's Career Center.

Interstride

If you are wondering how to find companies that are willing to sponsor your work visa, then Insterstride is just for you! This is a very useful job hunting website for international students, since it helps you look for companies which are willing to sponsor work visas. I recently found out this platform exists, and I am completing my last semester of my master's program. I regret that I did not know about this website earlier. You can also get some useful information about work visas such as which companies are willing to sponsor work visas.

Handshake

This is a job hunting platform which is designed for university students, where one can filter companies that will sponsor H1B visas and OPT visas. Job opportunities on this platform do not require much work experience. You also do not have to have any job experience. That is why this is such a friendly platform for university students and is one of the most popular job hunting platforms for college students, according to Handshake themselves. You might not find many companies that are international students-friendly, but I still recommend you use this platform, especially for those who are looking for an entry-level role.

My Tips for International Students

I have some tips for international students who are thinking of looking for a job in the U.S.. These tips are what I learned through my experience of looking for a job and an internship. I do not want other international students to suffer while hunting for a job and while collecting information about visas like me.

Start ASAP!

Starting job hunting early is a key and always good for you. You might think too early is not good, but it is better than having little time later. Being prepared will always help you. For example, if you know that the deadline of H1B visa is in March, you are able to start looking for a job early. I was not prepared at all until recently, and it was very overwhelming for me to collect the necessary information for visa applications, especially because I had to start them from scratch. Moreover, knowing other restrictions for international students is also important.

Other restrictions for international students:
1. If you work with an OPT visa after you graduate, you can only get a job(s) which is related to your area of study
2. You can be unemployed for the first 90 days with an OPT visa, but if you are unable to find a job after that, your visa will be void

*These restrictions can change

Visit your university's career center!

At the career center, you can talk to a staff member who can provide you with some useful tips for job hunting and career development. You can also ask the staff to check your cover letter and resume. Talking to the staff is free, and you can visit the office whenever you want (you need to make an appointment beforehand), so use the system as much as you can!

Start job hunting as soon as possible!

As I mentioned above, looking for a job takes a lot of time. What I was told by the staff at the career center was that job-hunting is like working, since it is time-consuming. I was also recommended at the career center to try to apply for at least 100 jobs. You cannot find a job within a day unless you are very lucky, so start looking for a job as soon as possible!

Attend career events!

There are some companies/institutions which sponsor H1B visas at career events. There are also some online events for international students regarding H1B visa and an OPT visa. This is also a good chance to build some connections with some companies!

Conclusion

Getting an internship and a job as an international student is tough and you need to put in so much time and effort. However, knowing some information about visas and some restrictions for international students can make a big difference. I advise you to always be prepared, and there is no "too early" to plan for your future career! I also advise that starting to start working on job hunting is a key for international students. It can be overwhelming, but there are many useful resources that can help you, such as an international office, and a career center. Use the available resources effectively, and do not hesitate to ask professionals if you have any concerns.

VIII
MONEY AND POLITICS:
THE PAID VS. UNPAID DEBATE
Deniz Guzeldere

Roadmap:
   i.   Introduction
  ii.   Paid Internships: Pros and Cons
 iii.   Unpaid Internships: Pros and Cons
 iv.   Conclusion

Key Takeaways:
- Are unpaid internships unfair?
- The advantages of both types of internships are important to consider.
- Weigh out pros and cons when deciding which internships to apply to.

"Important things to consider when being an unpaid intern is to make the best out of your experience, develop the skills you want to develop, and overall treat the internship with the same excitement and sense of responsibility that you would if it were paid."

Introduction

Should you get paid for an internship? Are unpaid internships immoral?

The debate over paid vs unpaid internships is frequently talked about among college students. The morality behind unpaid internships have been up for debate more recently as it may be seen as unfair or immoral to not pay interns. Many students might want to apply for an internship with an organization that they really like, but if it is unpaid it might sway them to not apply for it. There are many politicians who advocate for a more fair minimum wage, but will ignore the issue of unpaid internships or have unpaid interns themselves. It can be difficult to decide whether it is worth it to be an unpaid intern, depending on the company or organization. You might be able to attempt to negotiate to be paid when you are in the interview, but it can be difficult to bring it up especially when the position clearly states that it is unpaid. Unfortunately, there are not too many internship opportunities that offer some type of compensation, especially during the school year. But, if you start the search early for a summer internship you might be a little more lucky with finding a paid internship. Having a paid internship is great, but if you cannot get one that is okay because unpaid internships still have a lot to offer. The rest of this chapter will go into detail of the paid versus unpaid internship debate, as well as the advantages and disadvantages of each.

Paid Internships: Pros and Cons

Paid internships have both pros and cons, and it is important to weigh all of them when deciding what type of internship you are going to apply for or perhaps deciding which opportunity might be better for you. The following section will discuss three advantages regarding paid internships, followed by three disadvantages.

The Advantages

Make some money!

The type of compensation for a paid internship may vary, as it can be in the form of a salary, hourly wage, or stipend. Also, the amount of compensation will depend on the company or organization you applied to, the industry, and the location. The majority of the time you will get paid the minimum wage, so in California, for example, the minimum wage is currently $15.50 and internships could pay anywhere from $15 an hour to $20 an hour, depending on how much money that organization makes. There are times where you might be in the dark about how much the internship you applied for pays, and are left to ask the awkward question in the interview. Luckily, in California a new state bill just passed that requires companies to state clearly on their job postings how much they will pay or the range of pay. If you are not in California and you are at the interview going back and forth about if you should ask about the pay, just go for it! Towards the end of every interview you will usually be asked if you have any questions for them, and that gives you a great opportunity to ask about the pay. It can be scary to ask because you might start to overthink that they might not hire you now because you asked, but this is not true and it is important that they are paying you fairly. But overall, just knowing that you are going to be paid is a huge advantage. If you are not working a regular job while being an intern, then being paid through the internship can help you with at least some living expenses, and can just give you extra money to have, or allow you to build your savings. It is important to have an understanding of what it means to earn your own money, especially when you are in college and having that experience through an internship is even better. Also, having a paid internship might make you more motivated in your tasks and overall lead to better productivity and growth. In general, it is important to keep in mind that depending on the organization you are applying to intern for will have an impact on whether or not they will pay you.

From internship to job offers

A paid internship is sometimes more valued than unpaid internships, especially by employers who are looking at your resume. They tend to view paid internships as more legitimate and serious, and therefore they will be more inclined to offer you an interview or the job you are applying for. Being a paid intern not only provides value to yourself, but also to your employer. The employer is investing in a paid intern and is therefore investing in their growth, so they will make sure that their intern is learning as much as they can and gaining valuable experiences. As mentioned previously, when you are being paid for your internship you might feel more responsible and therefore have a better work performance because you know that your work is a contribution to the company or organization. A paid internship can also help you in developing a sense of professionalism, since you are being paid for your work and you are expected to perform in a professional manner. But this does not only mean you are professional with your duties or tasks, but it can also mean dressing appropriately, meeting deadlines, and growing your communication skills with your co-workers. Overall, paid internships can increase your chances in job opportunities post-graduation because employers will see that you have had paid work experience in the field that you are applying to and have a good sense of professionalism.

Widening your network

A lot of times, paid internships usually provide better training and mentorship opportunities than unpaid internships. Paid interns tend to receive more hands-on training and experience, feedback, and support from their employers. This ultimately ties back into the value advantage because your employer has invested in you to help them and they want to make sure that you are gaining as many skills as possible. Having a paid internship will help you with real world experience in the field you are working for. You might work on a project either on your own or with co-workers, interact with important clients or partners, and collaborate with others in your field. This will also allow you to have more exposure to the industry that you are working in because there will usually be some type of event(s) that you help plan, or you will have the opportunity to network with other professionals. During these events or meetings that you might attend, gives you a great opportunity to network with all different kinds of people and organizations. This exposure helps the intern develop a better understanding of the industry as well as make connections with different people that they might not have met before, and ultimately you could land a job since you made these connections.

The Disadvantages

The competition

One of the biggest disadvantages of a paid internship is that they are less common, meaning there are fewer opportunities for students. This ultimately leads these internships to being more competitive. There will be a larger pool of applicants since it is more competitive and it will be important to make sure that you stand out so that you can be considered for an interview. As stated earlier, paid internships might be more available during a specific time of the year and this is usually during the summer. A lot of students like to have the summer to themselves and travel, go home, or sometimes they decide to take a summer class. It is important that you weigh out what you want to do that summer and if you are willing to sacrifice, for example, being away from home for the summer for an internship. If you are going to apply for a paid internship, it is important that you know how to stand out in the sea of resumes that the company will receive and that you are prepared for the interview.

No days off

Most of the time paid internships will come with a strict schedule, especially over the summer, and require more time commitment compared to unpaid internships. Usually the schedule is a lot more strict during the summer since employers know that you probably are not in school and so they expect you to commit more of your time. This can be challenging for students who might want to plan trips or spend their summer hanging out with friends, as they will have to learn how to find a balance. If the paid internship is during the school year, then this can be even more challenging for students who are full time and have other commitments. If you know that there might be some clashes in your schedule with the internship then it might lead the employer to be more inclined to not hire you, only because they want someone who is available during all the hours and days they are asking for. Also, a lot of these paid internships are on-site or in a hybrid format, which can limit the intern if they do not have a car or if they prefer to work remotely. Finally, paid internships usually offer less flexibility in terms of time off, this includes vacation or sick days.

The pressure

The employer of a paid intern will usually have higher expectations for their intern, they will expect more from them, and this can add pressure or stress for the intern. As mentioned in the advantages sections, these employers are investing in you and will have high expectations so you will need to be prepared for that type of pressure. Along with this there will also be a high expectation of professionalism, this can mean in the sense of dress code, attending meetings and/or events, and communicating with your employer and co-workers in a professional manner. Because there will be higher expectations, you might be given assignments or projects that have specific deadlines or requirements. Also, with some of these internships the organization or company might view it as a trial period for a potential job opportunity which can cause a lot of stress on an intern.

Unpaid Internships: Pros and Cons

Unpaid internships also have their own pros and cons, some of them overlapping a bit with those of paid ones. Important things to consider when being an unpaid intern is to make the best out of your experience, develop the skills you want to develop, and overall treat the internship with the same excitement and sense of responsibility that you would if it were paid.

<u>The Advantages</u>

Getting a feel for the field

As stated in the paid internship section it can be difficult to find good paid internships, but there are plenty of unpaid internships making them less competitive. Since unpaid internships are less competitive, it is also less stressful on students to secure an internship in the field that they want. There will also be a wider variety of opportunities offered and a wider range of industries and organizations to apply to, like smaller business, non-profit organizations, or start-up companies. Although the organizations might not have the budget to have paid interns, the interns will get to experience working with the type of industry they are more interested in, which could be more valuable than being a paid internship with a type of company or organization that you do not see yourself working for in the future. Unpaid interns might also be more motivated to make solid connections and build strong relationships with their employer and co-workers, especially in smaller companies that have fewer staff. This also helps with building your communication skills especially with those superior to you. Although it might seem like there are not that many opportunities with an unpaid internship, it depends on how you decide to approach it.

Hybrid, in the office, or remote- it's your choice!

In an unpaid internship, the employer is not monetarily investing in their intern and thus are more willing to accommodate to your schedule. Unlike paid internships, unpaid internships are a lot more flexible in terms of scheduling as well as location and usually only require part-time work. You might be able to work remotely or in a hybrid format and you will likely be able to pick and choose the days/hours that you want to work. This makes it a lot easier on students who might be full time at school or have other personal commitments. Also, there might be some really valuable unpaid internships that are not in the same city or state that you live in but offer a remote option which allows you to have an option to apply to that internship. Overall, depending on your school schedule, extracurricular activities, etc, an unpaid internship is great in the sense that they are very flexible with students and do not have a strict schedule like paid internships.

Be the leader of your own projects

Since unpaid internships tend to have less structure and formalized tasks, the intern may have a better opportunity to pursue self-directed projects or explore other areas of interest within the organization or company. This helps the intern receive a more well-rounded experience and it can help them figure out what they might be more or less interested in and really help them with their career goals. Unpaid internships can also offer more learning opportunities, since the intern is not being paid then they will be more motivated to learn as much as they can and gain as much experience as possible. There are also times when the intern might have the chance to work with senior level staff, which allows them to connect with the senior level staff and grow a strong relationship with them. Having a well rounded experience and gaining the motivation to learn also helps the intern build their resume and prepares them for future job opportunities.

The Disadvantages

No money, more problems

Probably one of the biggest disadvantages of an unpaid internship is that there is no compensation, only experience. This is especially challenging on students who need to support themselves financially, and perhaps work while also going to school. Since they are not being paid, this can increase the interns living expenses in different ways. They may need to pay for public transportation or gas for their car to go to the internship site, they might need to buy new professional attire if they do not already have any, as well as other expenses. The financial burden is also hard on students who have to take out loans because if they are accepting an unpaid internship then they will probably have to take out additional loans in order to cover their financial obligations. Also, unpaid internships can create a lack of diversity since usually only students who can afford to work without pay are able to participate. This limits the pool of potential interns and maintains inequality in the workplace. It is important for students to seriously take into consideration whether they can afford to be an unpaid intern or not, as it is a very important factor in deciding the type of internship you are going to apply for.

Sometimes you'll be underappreciated

Unpaid internships can lack validation compared to paid internships, especially by future employers. Since the intern is not being paid, there are times where the supervisor or other staff members might not appreciate or give the intern credit for the work that they have done. In a similar sense, future employers may not view the intern's work as seriously or give them the same credit as they would to someone who was a paid intern and could disway them from hiring that person who was an unpaid intern. Also, since the company or organization is not paying the intern, they might not invest as much time and resources into training for the intern which can limit the intern's opportunity to gain valuable skills. Although an unpaid internship is not viewed with the same value as a paid internship, one way to make it more valuable is by taking the steps to ensure that they are treated seriously and given credit for their hard work.

Time and resources can be scarce

As stated multiple times in the previous sections, the company or organization is not investing in their intern and thus they might be less invested in the professional development of an intern than they are in the development of their paid employees. It will also be difficult for unpaid interns to have their voices and opinions heard even though it could be very valuable. But this is not to say that you should stay quiet the entire time you are an intern. It's important that organizations and companies start to include their interns in more meetings or in general acknowledge their work. Since unpaid interns are not viewed as essential as a paid employee, this can result in fewer mentorship opportunities as time and resources may not be set aside for the development of the intern. Finally, unpaid internships can sometimes be shorter in duration than paid internships, which can limit the intern in the amount of time they have to build strong relationships with their mentors and co-workers.

Conclusion

Overall, the debate between paid versus unpaid internships is one that comes with a lot of pros and cons on both sides. Throughout this chapter we have gone over three disadvantages and advantages for both unpaid and paid internships. There is some overlap between the two, but that is expected and is to show that if you are applying to two amazing internships and one is paid and the other is not, then that might be the only thing you have to weigh out.

Regardless, it is important to weigh out everything when deciding which internship positions to apply to, or which one you are going to accept. It is also important to note that the advantages and disadvantages that were listed in the previous paragraphs are not the only ones, and that they are not the same for every single type of internship. The day to day tasks of an intern can vary depending on the organization, but always expect that you will be helping somebody or multiple staff members on the days you work. Tasks can include researching, drafting up emails, helping set up events, and much more. During your interview you should not be afraid to ask what your day to day tasks would look like so that you can get a better idea of what the internship will be like. As a student, no matter if you are unpaid or paid, you should treat the internship as though it is your job as it will make you a better employee.

IX
VOICES OF INTERNS: LISTENING TO CURRENT INTERNATIONAL RELATIONS INTERNS
Erin Dwyer

Roadmap:

Key Takeaways:
- Focus on making connections.
- Internships are a great way to actually figure out what you love.
- Take initiative and advocate for yourself; it is worth asking if you can have more or less of any specific task.
- Never be afraid to ask questions, after all you are learning!
- Be ready to pivot, adapt, and fine tune some new skills.

"I could tell, by talking with Deniz, that the internship wasn't simply a job, but something she was passionate about, and truly enjoyed giving her time and effort to."

Going into the professional sphere for the first time, not knowing what to expect, getting an entry level internship in the field that you have been working towards, and meeting people who you look up to can be a really scary and daunting time. Everyone's experience will be different as you get into these internships and work with these different organizations. All of the authors of this book have their own story to tell, based on how their internships went, so this chapter is a chance to not only get to know some of the other authors a bit more, but also give you--the reader--a glimpse into what you could expect as you are on your own journey into the world of international relations.

Randy Reyes: Communications Intern at the Office of Immigrant Affairs for the City of San Diego

As I was talking with Randy, I learned that the issue of immigration policies is something that means a lot to him, as his parents are immigrants from Mexico, and he grew up in San Diego, a binational city. Therefore, he was always acutely aware of the immigration situation at the San Diego-Tijuana border. I could tell from speaking with him that Randy is pursuing a career in international relations in order to help others, and that he wants to make an impact on the lives of people who may be following a similar trajectory that his family did. Although immigration is a priority for him and his career goals, Randy is also notably interested in other issues like security and climate, all three of which he sees as implicitly intertwined within one another.

Randy was an intern from June to December 2022 with the City of San Diego's Office of Immigrant Affairs. He originally found an internship through University of San Diego's weekly internship email list for the Mayor's Office of Global Affairs, but due to some switches in the organization he ended up doing his internship in the newly created Office of Immigrant

Affairs instead. The Office was created for immigrants and refugees in San Diego to have access to resources that would assist in all sorts of civic, economic, and social integration. A lot of their work also focuses on creating strong communities for these families and businesses that are not only safe and inclusive but also culturally vibrant. This is a relatively new office, and Randy's internship primarily focused on the digital sphere and social media, a position that a lot of college students will see when applying for internships, especially considering many of these organizations have been pushing to become more digitized and capture an audience that is increasingly gaining their information online.

Randy on what a typical day looked like and his responsibilities:

Like I mentioned previously, Randy's main responsibility was to draft social media content and manage the office's social media platforms on Twitter, Facebook and Instagram. There was a lot of oversight with his social media drafts from his boss, especially at the beginning. He would present three different post options for his supervisor to look over and choose from. They would contain everything: from the caption to the graphics--often he would even design his own images. Then, once the final product was approved, he would post it online.

Randy would diligently read the news to see if there was any relevant immigration information, as well as review the Department of Homeland Security, and United States Citizen and Immigration Services newsrooms for federal policy updates. He would also conduct research for monthly newsletters that would be sent out to community leaders and stakeholders. Further into the internship he shadowed the press secretaries and digital media managers for the mayor, allowing him to attend a lot of unique, important, and interesting events, as well as expand his role in the position. Some of the things he would do included: take pictures for social media, serve as a notetaker, and work as a communications advisor for his executive director during media interviews.

Randy on the highlight of his internship:

For Randy, it was all of the amazing people he got to meet, including many leaders in the world of foreign and immigrant affairs. He sat in on a meeting with his boss (the Executive Director of Immigration Affairs), the Director of Global Affairs, San Diego Mayor Todd Gloria, and the United States Acting Assistant Secretary of State for Global Public Affairs to discuss San Diego's role as a border city and the current global migration challenges. He also got to meet Eva Millona, the USCIS Chief of Citizenship, Partnerships, and Engagement (United States Citizenship and Immigration Services), as well as other local USCIS officials, as he, the Executive Director of Immigrant Affairs, and the Deputy Director of Government Affairs sat down with Ms. MIllona and her staff to discuss ways San Diego could incentivize its immigrant communities to become naturalized U.S. citizens. Later, he also sat in on a meeting with officials from the UN High Commission for Refugees: U.S. Director of Strategic Communications, the External Relations Officer for Western Hemisphere Migration, and U.S.-Mexico Border Refugee Lead. Being able to attend these events and meet all of these individuals not only provided many new and exciting experiences for Randy, but they also opened the door to networking and having the opportunity to foster connections that very likely will be useful once he steps foot in the world of international affairs as a postgraduate.

Randy also highlights some of his own personal accomplishments. As the public is moving towards increasing the digitization of information--making it more accessible-- being able to verify yourself on social media is essential for garnering any authority. Randy was able to verify all three social media accounts during his time in the internship-- which again was for a new organization--he redesigned and relaunched the monthly newsletter, assisted with creating new logos and played a key part in making the image of this organization professional and its information easy to access.

At the end of his internship, he started helping put together a community event. Randy talked about how the immigrant community has a stigma against any government organization, and a lot of them do not know much about local politicians and the resources that are available to them. So his team started to put together an event that would allow the migrant community to engage with the city leaders and show them the different sorts of legal services available to them through a "know your rights"or "citizenship" workshop, in all different languages. The event would also help explain to migrants how to do essential tasks like paying for your water or electric bills, that are often left to the migrants to figure out.

Randy on the challenges he faced at his internship and how he overcame them:

Since these sorts of responsibilities were relatively new to Randy, he did have to know how to use other applications he was not very familiar with. For instance, for social media posts, he would create original graphic design concepts using Canva. He faced some challenges learning how to navigate the website and figuring out the best ways to produce the content he wanted to. He had used it for a school project before, but his internship really pushed him to use Canva to its full potential. It did take some trial and error, but after using it consistently for all the social media drafts, learning more about it online, and by asking his friends who used it all the time for presentations, Randy was able to become an expert with Canva. This allowed him to have more artistic freedom, and become more efficient in his tasks. Becoming adept with Canva was a great skill for Randy to learn as it will not only help him in his graphic design skills as an intern for this organization, but also is a skill that he can use moving forward in other positions.

Randy reflecting on his internship experience:

One of Randy's biggest pieces of advice--that I believe is worth highlighting again--is to never burn bridges, and focus on making connections. That means, when you go to meetings, no matter who is there, always be friendly with all the staffers, you never know who you will be talking to, and how they will matter to you down the line. With that, Randy emphasizes not to be afraid to ask questions, one of the main reasons you are there is to learn. Asking for help is not a bad thing, and often will really aid you in the future.

Overall, Randy loved the internship and found that it really impacted him and his studies. It showed him a new possible pathway in his future: focusing on the communication side of international relations and public service. Like working as a Digital Media Manager, a Press Secretary, Communications Manager/Director, or Strategic Communications Advisor. He thinks that media relations, social media strategies, public relations, and messaging is super important in the world of international relations. As it allows us to share and distribute the correct information about policy changes, new programs and services, and any other relevant news occurring that impacts constituents across the country and world.

To leave you with some last words from Randy: "I am super grateful that I was able to work at City Hall and that Justice for Mexico ended up canceling my internship. I think these type of things do happen for a reason because thanks to my internship at City Hall more specifically at the Mayor's Office, I have a solid network that is only continuing to grow, but I also have a full time job as a Community Representative and Social Media Manager for Councilmember Jennifer Campbell, Council District 2.

Deniz Guzeldere: Program Intern at the San Diego Diplomacy Council

Deniz is very passionate about working for a nonprofit organization (NGO) abroad in the future. She is from two very different cultural backgrounds and has a lot of knowledge about international relations. On top of English, she is a native Spanish and Turkish speaker, with education experience in French. During her college education, she focused much of her research on Turkey, U.S. relations with Turkey, strategic issues in Europe, and NATO.

She was an intern for the NGO San Diego Diplomacy Council, from September 2022 to February 2023. Deniz found her internship through LinkedIn because she connected with this organization by attending their Spring fundraiser in April 2022. She got to meet a lot of different people, which made her interested in learning more about what they do at SDDC and how to get involved. This organization is a non-profit, non-partisan organization designed by the United States Department of State to deliver programs and services that allows San Diego to connect and participate in the international sphere, specifically looking at challenges like: citizen safety, economic opportunity, social justice and environmental sustainability. Deniz helped with researching information for the various groups with the International Visitors Leadership Program (IVLP). A large majority of her job was centered around research, an area that could potentially be a primary responsibility for a lot of interns in other positions.

Deniz on what a typical day looked like and her responsibilities:

Deniz's internship was actually a hybrid format, so during the week, half of the time she would go into the office and the other half she would be online. The State Department would send her team a list of what the next upcoming IVLP group was focusing on. One of the those she handled was interested in economics, she would research the best organizations to reach out to, and send them emails to see if they could meet with the group.

The longer she stayed in her internship, she was able to make those best matches more quickly, and build connections with new organizations so that it would be easier to reach out to them in the future. Then once all the research and communication was set up, Deniz would make a program book, send it to the State Department and get it approved for the visitors. For the event itself, and the days leading up to it, she would also bring in any needed interpreters, and would staff a few of the events, meetings with the fellows, and sit in during the meetings. The fellows/attendees were usually in the mid 20's to late 30s's and came from all sorts of different countries, some were from different areas of Europe, a lot from South East Asia, Iraq and sometimes even India and Argentina. The groups themselves ranged from around 5 fellows to 20 fellows. Deniz was able to really learn a lot about event planning, while simultaneously tuning her research skills. Her team worked together to set up these events under the approval of the state department, and she was very hands-on throughout the entire process, allowing her to be a major player in running these events.

Deniz on the highlight of her internship:

For Deniz, her biggest accomplishment was as she was leading an IVLP project, and sending out emails to different organizations to ask if they would meet with the fellows, every organization that Deniz reached out to was more than happy to meet and come speak with the group. This accomplishment really shows the strength of the connections that Deniz made with these organizations during her time in the internship as well as her effectiveness in researching and finding that perfect match. This sort of time, effort, and skill behind the scenes is what makes these events not only so successful, but memorable for the fellows. It is also a testament of just how far Deniz has come during her time there, from a brand new recruit, who didn't know much about the organization, to someone who is a key player in running an entire event is extremely impressive.

But one highlight that just stood out to me, was that she also really just enjoyed her job, she liked what she did, she looked forward to staffing the various meetings. I could tell, by talking with Deniz, that the internship was not simply a job, but something she was passionate about, and truly enjoyed giving her time and effort to. This internship taught her so much, but also helped her focus on an area of international relations that she could see herself doing as a career. She cared about her work and I think that is something that every intern really wants at their position.

Deniz on the challenges she face at her internship and how she overcame them:

For Deniz, one of her biggest challenges in the beginning of her internship was learning all the different acronyms and attempting to figure out how everything is run and should be done. This is something that may be a big hurdle for a lot of interns. When going into a new environment, especially with an organization that works closely with the state department, there is a very particular way that things need to be performed. With that, there is a lot to learn and familiarize yourself with, that may be very new. One example that Deniz ran into was having to remember a lot of new technical terms that her team used, which at the beginning can seem really daunting. Deniz overcame this challenge just with time and being constantly exposed to it, especially as she took on more group projects, all the information eventually just stuck. Deniz was also not afraid to utilize her resources. For instance on her first day, she was given different word documents explaining all the various fellowships and that really helped her get the hang of things. She also was not afraid to ask for help. She would meet with her boss if she could not find an organization that would fit the groups needs and wants, she would also go to her boss and get feedback about all of her work, allowing her to really get the hang of the system and figure out how to jump through all of the governmental hoops.

Deniz on how her opinion was valued in the internship:

For Deniz, at the start of her internship, she did not typically share her opinions, especially as she was getting acclimated to the environment, and feeling out her position in the team. But as she got to know the team, as the newness of everything wore away and she felt more confident with the tasks that she needed to do, she really started to open up and speak her mind. When she did, Deniz said that everyone there was not only open to listening to what she had to say, but respected her opinions.

During Deniz's time, the organization also just started having interns be involved in staff meetings on Tuesday mornings, and that allowed the other team to see what she was contributing, it made her feel more like she was an equal. She would present updates on what she was working on and would also hear about what others were working on as well. She participated in open conversations about where to have events or suggested types of organizations that another staff member needed help with. I think that it can be hard to not have imposter syndrome especially when you are just starting out. But Deniz found that her internship really highlighted the impact she makes, and gave her the space to not only share her opinion but have her opinion be a valuable part of the conversation. It allowed her performance in her own work to improve, as well as the ways she can provide support for other team members.

Deniz reflecting on her internship experience:

If Deniz were able to give a piece of advice for new interns it would be, to not be afraid to ask questions. Deniz said that although it can feel daunting coming into a new environment, and she herself felt a bit shy, she found that everyone in her office was so nice, extremely welcoming and only wanted to help. Your supervisors, and co-workers are there to work with you, not against you, so you should never be afraid to go to them if you need any help. This is a very constant theme across my discussions with all the authors, which should be a tell on how important this is. Asking questions, admitting that you need help, not going at it alone, will benefit you, your employers as well as your future time there at the internship.

Lastly I do want to end Deniz's section by adding one more additional comment from her: "This internship was overall a great experience and I've learned so much from it. Prior to the internship I didn't know about the different fellowships that SDDC works with, and helping with the research and steps to organize the fellows time here was really interesting to me."

Madaleine Domingo: U.S Department of State: Virtual Student Federal Service Intern, EducationUSA Russia

Madaleine has dual citizenship with the United States and the United Kingdom. She is the daughter of an English immigrant mother and a Filipino father, and has had many experiences abroad. During her time at USD, Madaleine enrolled in a study abroad program called, Semester at Sea, where she traveled to 13 European countries while simultaneously taking college courses. Prior to Semester at Sea, Madaleine studied abroad in Madrid, Spain at the University of San Diego's international campus! Throughout these experiences, she discovered her passion for intercultural communication and committed to her career pursuits in diplomacy. Her experiences abroad cultivated her interests in migration patterns, refugee crises, and human rights issues around the world. She hopes to one day utilize her skills and experience as a U.S. Foreign Service Officer.

Madaleine interned for the U.S. Department of State: Virtual Student Federal Service Intern, EducationUSA Russia, which focused on international education. She worked there from August 2022 to May 2023. Madaleine always knew she wanted to work for the State Department, so she signed up for email subscriptions for internship opportunities in the State Department well before her internship search. In July 2022, the Virtual Student Federal Service (VSFS) program sent her an email notifying her that their application processes had opened. VSFS interns for EducationUSA Russia teach about American culture through American short stories, and literary devices. Madaleine helps to improve the student's English language skills while aiding some students in their college applications to the United States. Madaleine's help does not guarantee college acceptance, but it does provide a lot of information and exposure about college in the U.S. from a relevant perspective. The VSFS program is competitive, and EducationUSA Russia is one specific program within VSFS that fosters international connection between Russia and the United States.

Madaleine on what a typical day looked like and her responsibilities:

Madaleine had a lot of day-to-day freedom but also had to do a lot of planning: she designed her own lesson plans, she led the meetings, met with students one-on-one, and decided how her classes ran as well as what she taught them. Madaleine did have some guidance going through training sessions three times a semester on how to effectively teach online. As a VSFS intern, Madaleine had two responsibilities to two different groups: Pre-Competitive College Club (Pre-CCC) members, and Competitive College Club (CCC) members. Madaleine hosted bimonthly English language classes to the younger learners (Pre-CCC members). They were about an hour and a half long per session. She started it off with a check in activity, some ice breakers, and then she asked someone to give a plot summary of what happened in the short story that they had to read for the class. She then lectured about the author of the short story and went through discussion questions the students answered as homework before they met each session. Madaleine then dived into the analysis of the short stories' context in the greater scheme of American culture and core values and discussed specific literary devices. At the end, she wrapped up the class with reflection questions and a song of the month that corresponded with the themes of the short story. Madaleine is a firm believer of bodily movement in her classes to stimulate learning, which is why she incorporated stretching and dancing to the song of the month into her sessions. This formatting she came up with herself, and every session was watched by her mentor who gave her feedback.

Madaleine was also responsible for doing weekly meetings with students who were applying to U.S. colleges (CCC members). She would help them with their college applications to the U.S., answer their questions, and host webinars about how to craft personable and successful college essays and personal statements. She really built a strong personal connection with these members, and would often meet with them one on one, as well as follow up with them about where they got accepted and where they wanted to go. Madaleine could tell just how grateful the students were for this experience by how involved they got and how much they took advantage of the opportunities she gave them.

Madaleine on the highlight of her internship:

Madaleine kindly talked about her additional responsibility when she was asked to host her first webinar on how to craft meaningful and clear college application essays for graduate students. Attendees told Madaleine that her sessions were the most useful and engaging sessions in the program so far. Their positive feedback really struck Madaleine as something that she will always remember. Being able to make a noticeable impact for her students, and see them be excited and grateful is something that made me smile just listening to her describe it.

Madaleine loves working with the CCC members since they have so many big aspirations to study and pursue their dreams in the United States. She is able to interact with them on a personal level while learning about their passions and goals. Madaleine enjoyed her job and she truly cared about her students. Being able to have this sort of opportunity as a college student was extremely fulfilling for her.

Madaleine on the challenges she faced at her internship and how she overcame them:

For Madaleine, the biggest challenge for her was the time change in Russia, and being able to connect with her students as frequently as she would have wished. She would have to wake up very early on weekdays and weekends, and schedule sessions three weeks in advance. This challenge made Madaleine learn strong time management skills. Being able to fit your schedule with individuals in a completely different time zone across the world is not easy for a full time student. But, Madaleine's students were eager to get her help, and with some adjustments, she was able to overcome that bump in the road, and make the many following months easier.

When Madaleine was confronted with a task that she found to be particularly challenging, she asked for help. Not only through her mentors, but she also reached out to the previous interns who were in the program last year. Previous interns are a great resource that everyone should consider since they were in the same shoes as you not very long ago.

The last thing I do want to mention is how Madaleine overcame any language barriers which is something that you may have to face in international relations internships. For Madaleine, she had to be sure and speak slowly and articulate her words, which could be a bit of a challenge at first. But, all of her students had a great foundational English level, and Madaleine's job was to improve those skills while educating about American culture through short stories. Her internship involved a lot of patience and moments of adaptation amidst many networking opportunities. All of this led her to be a very successful teacher, mentor and intern in this organization.

Madaleine on how her opinion was valued in the internship:

Madaleine did find that her opinion was very valued in her internship. All of the interns would actually meet once a month to debrief about the sessions, make any changes that were needed, and give feedback to each other. Since they were college students, and the internship was focused around helping others get into colleges, their opinions were well received from their mentors. Madaleine said that the mentors were all about improving the program, and were really open to hearing any suggestions, in fact, they encouraged any feedback.

Having this sort of strong, open, and trusting environment was really beneficial for Madaleine to not only improve her own sessions, but also to improve how the program is run in general. Since she was in the internship for almost one year,

Madaleine was able to encounter a lot of different and new situations, build trust with her mentors, and watch how any changes impacted the overall outcome of the program.

Madaleine reflecting on her internship experience:

Madaleine had some really great advice for other individuals seeking internships in really any organization: if you are looking for ways to get your foot in the door with large organizations, signing up for email subscription is the way to go. That way, you can stay up to date with the unique opportunities available to you.

VSFS is run by the U.S. State Department, and for Madaleine, being a registered intern in the State Department's is a big step in the door for the future. The government has a record of her work, and the people she worked with during her time in the internship could potentially end up being people she sees on her first day on the job, or on an interview panel for a full time position.

To finish Madaleine's section I do have a final quote from her: "I will always cherish the many memories I have with my mentees and EducationUSA Russia administrators. Throughout my experience in the program, I feel like I have greatly accelerated my intercultural communication skills which I know will aid me in my endeavors in the Foreign Service".

Conclusion

At the very beginning of this chapter, I talked with Randy who was a Communications Intern at the Office of Immigrant Affairs for the City of San Diego. He discussed what it was like to run the organization's social media page, be in the room with many city and federal leaders, as well as be a part of a team that runs community events. He gave some great advice about building connections, and not being afraid to ask questions.

My interview with Deniz was centered around her internship as a Program Intern at the San Diego Diplomacy

Council. Her internship focused more on the research side of international relations. She talked about what it was like to actually plan an event for individuals coming from other countries, and how the team dynamic was really welcoming to her as an intern. Deniz got first hand experience working with government agencies and their protocols, which was a challenge at first, but is information that will be extremely useful for her in the future.

The last author I had the opportunity to interview was Madaleine who worked for the U.S. Department of State as a Virtual Student Federal Service Intern, EducationUSA Russia. Madaleine's internship was such a unique experience in that she actually got to teach Russian students and help them with their application to United States universities, creating unique and strong relationships with them. Madaleine talks about great ways to seek help and advice as an intern, as well as how she navigated a position that gave her a lot of freedom.

Each of the authors I interviewed for this chapter all have various experiences, highlights, challenges and advice that are more applicable to you than you might think. Even if you find yourself in a completely different position than these three authors, there is still so much to learn from their stories.

WORKS CITED

"About CSIS." *Center for Strategic and International Studies,* https://www.csis.org/about.

"About IBA." *City of San Diego: Office of the Independent Budget Analyst,* https://www.sandiego.gov/iba/aboutus.

"About: Justice in Mexico." *Justice in Mexico,* https://justiceinmexico.org/about/.

Eads, Audrey, et al. "21 Helpful Internship Tips for Success (With Importance)." *Indeed,* https://www.indeed.com/career-advice/starting-new-job/internship-tips.

"H-1B Visa: Step by Step Guide." *Prodigy Finance,* https://prodigyfinance.com/resources/blog/h1b-visa-guide/.

Loretto, Penny. "Key Qualities of a Good Internship." *The Balance,* https://www.thebalancemoney.com/how-to-define-a-good-internship-1986795.

Smith, Jacquelyn. "15 Ways To Stand Out As An Intern." *Insider,* https://www.businessinsider.com/15-things-interns-do-to-stand-out-2014-5.

Vivian, Nikki. "10 Important Qualities of an Effective Intern." *CareerAddict,* https://www.careeraddict.com/top-10-qualities-of-an-effective-intern.

Ziebart, Sydney. "Bring Positive Attitude, Work Ethic to Internships." *University of Wisconsin Oshkosh: Department of Journalism,* https://uwoshjournalism.wordpress.com/2022/04/27/bring-positive-attitude-work-ethic-to-internships/.

CONTRIBUTORS

Madaleine Domingo is from the California Bay Area and is a senior at the University of San Diego, graduating with a bachelor's degree in political science and communication studies. Madaleine currently is an intern for the U.S. Department of State with EducationUSA Russia, teaching about American culture and core values through short stories and literary devices. She discovered her passions for international education, intercultural communication, and human rights activism during her junior year studying abroad in Spain and on Semester at Sea. In the fall of 2023, Madaleine will travel to Thailand as a Fulbright grantee where she hopes to kickstart an international career in foreign service!

Erin Dwyer is completing her third year at University of San Diego, and is studying political science with the intention of going to law school following her undergraduate education. Erin was adopted from China when she was a baby and grew up in the Pacific Northwest in Washington State. Erin was a legal intern at the Southern California Immigration Project, assisting the attorneys in the firm who were representing asylum seekers from Africa. She has always been passionate about a future career in law since she was very young and her time in this internship has opened her eyes to the interconnectedness and potential future career with the legal field and international relations.

Deniz Guzeldere is of Turkish and Mexican descent and was raised here in San Diego. She grew up visiting her dad's family in Istanbul, Turkey every summer and visits her mom's family regularly in Mexicali. Deniz is currently a Program Intern at the San Diego Diplomacy Council, where she researches and organizes different International Visitor Leadership Programs (IVLPs) that are hosted here in San Diego. Deniz graduated in May 2022 with a Bachelor of Arts in International Relations from the University of San Diego. She is very passionate about Turkish foreign policy, NATO, and the EU and has focused the majority of her undergraduate as well as graduate work on these topics.

Ryan Haile is currently enrolled at University of San Diego in a concurrent Juris Doctor and Masters of Arts in International Relations. He is just finishing his second year, and has two more years until he receives both degrees. He holds a bachelor's degree in Political Science and a minor in Theology also from University of San Diego. He enjoys watching sports, reading great literature, and following current events and the news. He was born and raised in San Diego, California, and plans to practice Tax law and Trusts & Estates law. He will be working at Qualcomm in their compliance department working on export controls in summer 2023.

Amanda Mueller is originally from the San Francisco Bay Area, and she graduated from the University of San Diego in 2022 with a Bachelor's Degree in Political Science. Through the combined BA/MA program, she has continued to work toward her Master's Degree in International Relations. Within this program, she has written extensively on politics and security in sub-Saharan Africa, focusing on the causes and the spread of military coup d'etats. Amanda is currently an intern with the San Diego County Sheriff's Department, but before this internship she worked as a preschool teacher for two years.

Saleena Ordorica received her B.A. in International Relations and Sociology with a concentration in Law, Crime, and Justice from the University of San Diego in 2022 and will soon be graduating with her M.A. in International Relations. She is now currently working as a research intern for the San Diego World Affairs Council and hopes to begin a career with the intelligence community after graduation. Her interests lie in analyzing the continuously evolving threats posed to our national security and formulating comprehensive strategic policies to effectively combat them. She is passionate about diminishing the influence of organized crime groups in regions where more vulnerable populations are the primary targets of this physical harm and violence. She also has a strong background in leadership and has worked directly with undergraduate students as both a mentor and tutor to support these individuals both academically and professionally.

Randy Reyes is currently serving as the Community Representative and Social Media Manager for San Diego City Councilmember Jennifer Campbell and oversees constituent services for the Point Loma and Midway communities. Randy graduated in May 2022 with a Bachelor of Arts in International Relations with a focus on international security from the University of San Diego, and is obtaining his Master of Arts in International Relations with a regional focus in Latin America. Randy is very passionate about international security, immigration policy, public diplomacy, and strategic communications and hopes to one day hold a job in the U.S. foreign relations field where he can combine his interests. Randy was born and raised in San Diego County and is the son of two Mexican immigrants who migrated from Michoacán, Mexico. As a first-generation child of migrants, he is proud to start his career in public service at San Diego City Council.

Sabrina Richards is a sophomore at the University of San Diego, graduating in two and a half years with a bachelor's degree in political science and a minor in law and ethics. Sabrina is from Las Vegas, Nevada. She interned for Congressman Darrell Issa in California's 48th Congressional District, aiding his constituents and helping conduct research for potential legislation. Sabrina has been passionate about politics for as long as she can remember, and she had a wonderful time learning first hand what it takes to run a district office successfully. She learned a great deal from her supervisors, Chris and Steven, and is thankful to Congressman Issa for the opportunity. Sabrina is simultaneously completing her master's in international relations, and upon completion, will attend law school in order to pursue a career in law!

Namie Yazaki is an international student from Japan. She graduated from Tokyo University with B.A. in Global Innovation Studies. Namie speaks Mandarin, Shanghainese, and French in addition to Japanese and English. She studied in Lille, France for one year during her undergraduate program, and enjoyed traveling around Europe and studying French. Her interests are in the relationship between media and politics, since she's fascinated by how media can shape people's political thoughts. Namie decided to study in a graduate program in the U.S. eight years ago when she was in high school, and here she is!